The

PLEASURE OF GARDENING

CREATING STYLE

The

PLEASURE OF GARDENING

CREATING
STYLE

*How to design and construct your
ideal garden*

A N D R E W   P F E I F F E R

ANAYA
PUBLISHERS LTD

CONTENTS

UNDERSTANDING YOUR GARDEN

ABOVE: *It is important to be aware of which parts of your garden get sun and shade, and at which times of the day. A pergola is a valuable asset as it produces shade at midday, but if designed well, will allow in light late in the afternoon.*

PREVIOUS PAGE: *When designing your own garden, look at mature gardens in your local area for inspiration. Here, the red rose bush and the blue door create an interesting contrast.*

Getting started

Imagine that you have recently moved into a new house around which there is very little garden, possibly just bare earth, and imagine also that you want to know something about gardening and garden design. How are you going to get the most from the opportunities that this valuable ground offers, and at the same time avoid expensive and time-wasting mistakes?

Firstly, spend a little time getting inspiration. Walk around your neighbourhood and look at any mature gardens. Make a note of things that you like and things that you do not. Visit your local botanic garden or any well established local garden open to the public and make a list of the plants that appeal to you. Visit local nurseries and garden centres and ask for their catalogues. You will soon learn which trees, shrubs, climbers and flowers thrive in your locality and this knowledge will stand you in good stead when you start to design and make your garden. Gardening is a pleasure with tremendous rewards, and in learning what plants grow well in your area you are helping to ensure future success.

Now think about your own garden and forget plants for a while. Which aspect do the various parts of your garden have? What time of day do they get the sun in the summer months, and how does

ABOVE: Many gardens made today are town gardens and tend to focus inwards. The clever design of this garden creates a tiny paradise in a limited space. Potted plants (gardenias, petunias, fuchsias and lilies) develop the pink, green and white colour theme.

this compare with the winter months? Which parts of your garden are the sunniest and which have the most shade? Knowing the answers to these questions is vital to the success of your garden, as very few plants can tolerate both full sun and full shade.

It is important that you get to know a little concerning your soil. Is it heavy or light, and does it therefore need breaking down or building up?

You should also be aware of the pH of your soil. pH is the term used to designate the acid or alkaline reaction of the soil. A pH reading of seven is neutral. Readings below seven denote acidity and from seven to fourteen they denote increasing alkalinity. Any good local nursery might be able to give you a reasonable idea as to whether your soil is neutral, acid or alkaline. If they cannot help, the herbariums of many botanic gardens will analyse a small sample for a modest fee. In any case, the issue only becomes critical if the pH of your soil happens to be either very acidic or very alkaline.

Having determined what type of soil you have, turn your attention to the surroundings of your house and garden and the view you get from them. The object of the garden has traditionally been to link the house to its natural surroundings. These days, however, when most gardens are in towns rather than the country, many are designed to hide or disguise the man-made surroundings. (These issues will be discussed in more detail in Chapter 5 in the section on small backyard gardens.) Stand in the centre of your garden and look at the horizon while turning in a 360 degree arc. Do you see a broad dome of sky overhead, or is it hidden here and there by nearby tall buildings? What do you like about the view and wish to retain and what do you dislike and want to hide?

One of the most important elements of landscape design is the turning of what initially appear as insurmountable disadvantages into advantages. An adjoining building that backs on to your garden might, for example, present a tall and windowless wall to your gaze. What can you do to hide this sheer cliff of masonry? One answer would be to design an interesting pattern of trellis-work, in either wood or metal, and fix it to the wall. If this doesn't have as much softening effect as you would wish, you could grow climbing plants like roses and clematis over the trellis, which will soften its outline without completely hiding it from view.

Now consider the view you get from each window of your house. Make a mental note of those windows that have an attractive outlook with aspects that you will wish to 'borrow', and those windows that look out on to a view that you wish to obscure by means of trees and shrubs. You should also take into account the architectural style of your house. This will dictate what type of garden you plant—formal or informal. A house with a symmetrical facade is already stating a strong case in favour of a formal garden, at least if the garden is close to the house. On the other hand, a formal garden may look out of place beside a house with a markedly asymmetrical facade or with curving, fluid walls.

One of the forces that will profoundly affect your future garden is climate. Is your climate temperate, subtropical, Mediterranean or desert? Not only will the answer to this question influence—or even dictate—the type of plants you use in your garden, it will also have a strong bearing on its ultimate layout and design. One of the advantages of gardening in the United States is that, horticulturally, the entire country has been divided into numbered climatic zones, the lower the number the colder the climate. Almost all nursery catalogues list plants according to the zones that each will tolerate. This system is not always fail-safe, but knowing which climatic zone you live in gives you a very good idea of which plants will thrive and which will either suffer or die.

By now you will have a good idea of the advantages and disadvantages of your land, and of its potential. The next thing to consider is how you actually intend to use your garden. What are your expectations? Jot them down on paper, starting with all those necessary but unglamorous items and objects you will have to put in your garden—a garden shed for tools and lawn mower, a compost heap, a vegetable garden, the clothes line, a dog kennel, parking space for cars, a drive leading to the garage and a small greenhouse. These are just some of the things you might consider. Now—a more exciting task—write down the ways in which you would like to relax in your garden, and what you will need to include for this purpose. Possibilities might include a lawn for the children to play games on, a barbecue, an herbaceous border, a swimming pool and a shaded area for outdoor dining.

You may now be faced with the prospect that you simply do not have enough space to realise all your ideals. In that case, you will have to number the items on your list in order of priority. One decision may force another: for example, a decision to have a lawn means finding space for a mower, unless, of course, you intend to pay someone to cut the lawn. Another distinct possibility is that you will decide that it is too expensive to carry out all projects at once and some, like installing a swimming pool, may have to be put on hold for a few years. In this case, it is important that the site for the swimming pool be determined at the outset. It would be wasting time and money to put the garden shed in the sunniest spot in the garden and then have to move it later because this is the ideal place for the pool.

Remember that no garden can be considered well designed if it does not function efficiently. And the smaller the garden the smaller your margin of error. You may decide, wisely, that you'd rather dry laundry in the sun than in a drying machine, in which case you will have to determine early on where to put the clothes line. It should be close to the laundry and receive direct sun for at least several hours per day. Once space has been allocated to serve a functional purpose like drying clothes, it makes sense to site any garden shed or greenhouse nearby. All these mundane items could then be screened from the rest of the garden by a wall, trellis or hedge.

Once you have decided where to site the working part of the garden—and how to hide it—you can then turn your mind to the design of the leisure part of the garden.

ABOVE: A smooth clipped lawn, surrounded by hedging and its borders blooming with plants of various heights, leads to a white garden seat. Look at the shape of your garden and think about how to create a sheltered space for such a seat.

The
ELEMENTS
OF DESIGN

Unity

People have been making gardens, and gardens of many different kinds, for thousands of years. Over all this time, certain elements of design have been universally regarded as important. All ultimately satisfying gardens, no matter what their period or style embody, to a greater or lesser degree, the following elements:

- unity
- scale
- mass and void
- light and shade
- time
- well-expressed associations.

Most art forms, including painting, sculpture and architecture, are given the licence to shock while still being regarded as great works. A garden that shocks ultimately fails. The art of landscape gardening is perhaps unique in that ultimate success depends upon how restful and refreshing to the spirit the garden is, however old-fashioned that notion may be. Gardens are composed principally of

OPPOSITE: Massing the same elements together in a bold design creates a strong sense of unity. In this lakeside grouping, the unity is strengthened by contrast—yellow flowers against a background of blue flowers.

PREVIOUS PAGE: The nasturtium weaves itself in and out of whatever structure it can find. Here, an ancient iron gate lends itself well to the trail of leaves.

ABOVE: The use of small hedging and a variety of groundcovers along this long and winding path creates a sense of unity.

plants, and plants, being living things, are constrained by the laws of nature, otherwise they die. A banana tree, for example, will not grow out of doors in Alaska. Above and beyond this, plants impose subtle expectations on the viewer that inanimate objects like paint, canvas, clay, stainless steel, bricks and mortar do not.

A garden achieves its restful and refreshing quality by means of unity. A garden composed of lawn and clumps of trees framing a view of a green valley has unity. Place a border of strongly contrasting flower colour between the garden and

the view and you draw the eye away from the view and direct attention to the flowers. The eye will shift restlessly between the brightly coloured flowers and the view and the sense of calm and unity will be lost.

There are many ways you can achieve unity in a garden. One is to base it on the existing ground form and surrounding native flora. This may not by itself result in a terribly exciting garden, but it will have the virtue of being restful.

The house or building around which the garden is to be made can impose a sense of unity if the ground plan of the garden complements the architectural style of the house. The proper use of tone and colour can unify a garden, as can imposing a strict colour scheme on the small garden.

Because most gardens these days are in towns, they tend to be inward looking, shutting out the world beyond their boundaries. In such gardens unity can be achieved by focusing attention on one single object like a fine tree or a fountain, and making it the dominant feature. On the other hand, if the garden has a view, unity is achieved by following the simple rule—the better the view the simpler the garden.

If you know what you want of your garden and carry out your intentions in a singleminded, straightforward way, your garden is more likely to have unity.

Scale

It is important that the proportions of a garden be related to the house or building it surrounds and that they take into account the scale of the human form. Where a garden looks out beyond its boundaries to the wider world, it is also important that the scale of the garden take into account its view.

A garden with clumps of trees and broad, sweeping lawns surrounding a small cottage will obviously be out of scale with the cottage, even though the clumps of trees may be in scale with the lawn. By creating the expectation of something grander, the broad lawns only serve to isolate the cottage and make it look lonely and out of context with the scale of the garden. A smaller lawn designed to bear a relationship to, and to be in proportion with the cottage will create a far greater degree of harmony.

In designing a garden terrace its dimensions will depend firstly on the scale of the house. A small house with a huge paved terrace attached will give the impression of being lost in a desert of paving. A larger house with a tiny terrace may look equally out of place. The dimensions of a terrace will depend also upon the purpose to which it will be put, and the number of people who might normally be expected to use it. If you plan to hold large dinner parties on the terrace, allow enough room around the table for the guests to be able reach their places without fear of falling into the swimming pool or stepping into a garden bed. Gardens should err slightly on the side of generosity of scale.

Although the dimensions of a garden remain static—unless more land is acquired—there are several means by which the apparent depth of a garden can be increased. One way is to plant large trees in the foreground and progressively smaller ones with increasing distance from the foreground. Much the same effect can be achieved by planting trees and shrubs with large leaves in the foreground, and placing those with increasingly smaller leaves behind. Using bright colours like red and orange in the foreground, contrasting with cooler colours such as blue and grey in shaded areas on the boundary of a small garden not only increases the apparent length of the perspective—due to the fact that light tones tend to come forward and dark tones to recede—but also tends to give the illusion of limitless space.

These methods are best suited to small gardens where the only vantage point might be a garden terrace or a window of the house. In larger gardens such methods are better avoided as they can produce the converse effect on the viewer who is at the opposite end of the vista looking back towards the house.

ABOVE:The scale of these smaller garden areas within the larger garden has been carefully planned so as to achieve a sense of harmony.

OPPOSITE: The apparent length of this vista has been increased by placing at its end a small statue that contrasts markedly with the tall slender gate.

Mass and Void

The basic pattern of all landscapes and gardens comes from the division of the garden into masses and voids. Masses are hills, trees, tall shrubs, walls, buildings etc.—in short any object of density seen above the line of sight. Voids are open spaces. Although these might include low flower beds and parterres they are, in particular, areas of grass and water.

Masses divide the voids around them, and give emphasis to them. A garden might, for instance, be composed of a large central lawn and from the house, you might see a clump of trees on the left and a neighbouring house on the right. The mass of the trees and the separate mass of the neighbouring house emphasise the 'void' of the lawn. If the mass, density or apparent weight of the clump of trees appears to be similar to the weight of the neighbouring house, then it can be said that a balance or harmony

LEFT: Masses are any objects of density seen above the line of sight. Here, in Vita Sackville-West's rose garden at Sissinghurst, the shrub roses on either side of the path (the void) are masses, counterbalancing each other.

has been created. In the same way, a small dense object like a low, dark, evergreen shrub might balance the density, or mass, of a large diffuse object like a tall, light-green and very open tree, provided the eye perceives them as having the same apparent weight.

The question of masses and voids is inextricably linked with scale. In the case of the small cottage framed by a huge lawn bordered by massive clumps of trees, the void of the lawn is in harmony with neither the clumps of trees nor the cottage, and the clumps of trees themselves are not in harmony with the house. In the garden there should be a balance not only between masses and voids, but also between one mass and another.

In colder climates it is important to remember that deciduous trees lose much of the weight and density of their mass as their leaves fall in the autumn. This is why conifers and other evergreen trees can play such an important role in the winter garden; their density remains constant and, consequently, although the balance between mass and void in the garden shifts because of the deciduous trees present, it will not shift so much as to destroy the harmony of the garden.

Light and Shade

Too much shade in a garden is liable to create a gloomy effect, whereas too much sun is harsh and overwhelming. Just as masses and voids need to be carefully balanced, so too do light and shade. The balance of light and shade that you strike in your garden will be strongly influenced by climate. Gardeners in cities with warm climates, like Sydney and Los Angeles, will plant to create pools of shade, whereas those in cities like London and Boston, with colder climates, will be biased in favour of the sun.

Certain effects of light and shade transcend the issue of climate. An object seen in sunlight through a pool of shade is always made more important and the scene thereby becomes more highly charged. An ornamental pool standing in sunlight becomes more appealing to the eye if it is seen through an intervening area of shade cast by surrounding trees. Likewise, the sensation of simply sitting in the shade of a group of trees and looking out at the sunlight beyond has a universal appeal regardless of climate. Although the mood of a garden is dictated more strongly by colour than by anything else, the orchestration of light and shade also has a powerful effect.

In those cooler climates where you can normally expect to have many overcast days, planting areas of yellow flowers like daffodils or forsythia can create the effect of pools of light. Similarly, in shady corners you can create the effect of dappled light by planting variegated groundcover plants and shade-tolerant variegated shrubs like the unfairly maligned aucuba.

LEFT: The orchestration of light and shade has a powerful effect on the mood of a garden. Here, the filtered light from the canopy of trees creates a cool and inviting area in which to relax.

Time

G arden design is unique amongst the arts, in that time, during which plants grow to maturity, plays such a vital role.

Formal gardens because of their clear-cut patterns of hedges, paths, rows of trees and pools can be appreciated, at least partially, from the start. Haphazard collections of plants arranged informally are much more dependent on time to develop any kind of recognisable form and, once mature, slide more quickly into chaos if neglected.

One of the pitfalls in designing a garden is not taking into account the eventual height and spread of the trees, shrubs, climbers and flowers chosen for the garden. Always consider carefully and plan for the mature size of any plant and allow for this in the layout, whether you are designing a garden to last for 30 years or 300.

LEFT: This plantation of birches and crab-apples has been carefully designed to create an immediate effect whilst the plants are comparatively young, and yet the trees have plenty of space in which to mature.

Well-expressed Associations

Colour in the garden runs the risk of making us blind to other fundamentally important design elements. When planning a garden it is better to think initially in black and white. Even though colour may end up being one of the most appealing features of your garden it is, by itself, one of the least important issues and should be one of the last to be addressed.

The shape, size and texture of the foliage of plants, and the way the foliage complements or contrasts with the leaves of other plants, is more important to the design of your garden than flower colour. Look at the shape and texture of the leaves of different plants, and the way shape and texture interact with each other, and aim to place greater emphasis on foliage rather than flower colour in the planting arrangements of trees, shrubs, climbers and flowers. Silhouetted against the sky, those hills of Rome not completely built over, provide striking examples of contrast—contrast between the dark needles of umbrella pines, the shiny light-green fronds of palms and the compact dense and almost deathly black foliage of the cypresses. The shapes of these trees, the spreading almost horizontal branches of the pines forming a domed canopy, the exotic fan shape of the palm fronds and the strongly vertical accents of the cypresses, contrast with and complement each other in an extraordinarily pleasing way.

In herbaceous borders, or beds of mixed flowers and shrubs that use several different flower colours mixed with the greens of the foliage, it is the colours of the flowers that catch your eye and hold your attention. In borders restricted to one flower colour, however, it is the shape and texture of the foliage that predominates, giving a calmer effect.

The pattern of the large formal gardens of the past was formed by means of hedges, lawns, rows of trees, stretches of gravel and bodies of water, and it was important to keep contrasts of texture relatively simple and straightforward. In many small contemporary gardens, which are greatly influenced by the Japanese tradition, the converse is true. Here a tremendous wealth of textural similarity and contrast—not only that of plants but also of stone, wood and water—can be built up into interesting patterns that are best appreciated at close quarters.

Association by ecological compatibility is almost inevitably successful, because everything that thrives in the same conditions looks right together. Rhododendrons, because they like a light acid soil, associate well with almost any heathland plant such as Scots pine (*Pinus sylvestris*) and birches, or with other acid-loving plants like primulas and Himalayan poppies.

ABOVE: Contrasting white, blue and pink flowers capture the attention. Complementing the flower colour and creating interest during the the flowerless months is the silver, dark green and light green foliage.
OPPOSITE: Vita Sackville-West's white garden at Sissinghurst is a masterpiece of contrasting shape and texture of foliage. This scene is a good example of well-expressed association.

USING
COLOUR

Creating the Mood

What the eye notices most in a garden is colour and, even though other factors are involved, the mood a garden creates is principally evoked by colour. In making a garden you are faced with a large number of options, amongst which are planting a broad range of flower colours, or limiting flowers to a monochromatic scheme, or simply using green, the most common garden colour of all. Whatever you decide to do will profoundly affect the mood of your garden.

Red, yellow and blue are called the primary colours, because all other colours can be formed from them. Purple, orange and green are secondary colours, so named because they result from a mixture of primary colours. You can derive tremendous pleasure learning about colour relationships by experimenting with tubes of red, yellow and blue water-paints.

Primary colours normally do not mix well in the garden. You have only to think of daffodils of pure primary yellow, for instance, clashing with pelargoniums of vermilion red, and of the same vermilion pelargoniums clashing with the sky blue of *Salvia patens*.

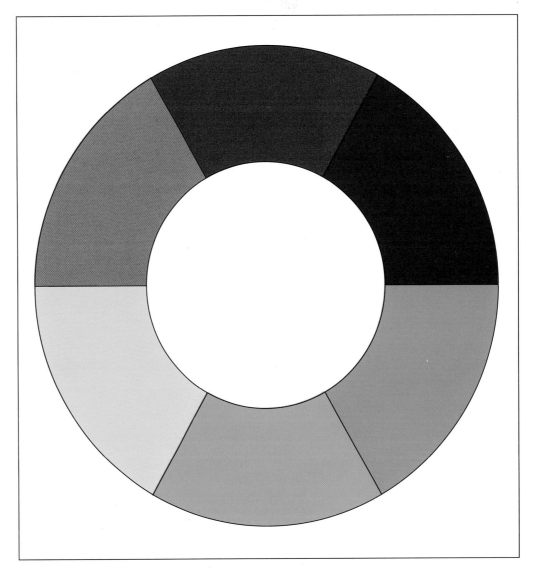

PREVIOUS PAGE: The mood of a garden is created principally by colour. Striking red bougainvillea seen against a steely dark grey background has a particularly powerful effect.

ABOVE: The primary colours are red, yellow and blue. Colours opposite each other on the colour wheel are complementary and provide the strongests contrasts, for example red and green, while colours close to each other on the wheel are harmonious, for example blue and purple.

OPPOSITE: One of the options open to the gardener is to limit the scheme to two colours. Here pure white flowers (candytuft) harmonise with creamy-white (violas) and yellow flowers (chamomile).

Colours that are opposite each other on the colour wheel are complementary—in other words they provide the strongest contrasts. An example of this is green, which contrasts strongly with red, its complementary colour. Colours closest to each other on the wheel are harmonious as, for instance, yellow and orange.

In general, aim to make the theme of a garden's colour scheme one of harmony rather than of contrast. Contrasts, especially where two complementary colours are equally represented, create powerfully disquieting effects. Seasonal contrasts, however, in which one colour is dominant, are capable of creating highly exciting effects. As a simple example of this, think of the red poppies that pepper the fresh spring grass in Mediterranean countries. When designing such contrasts yourself, make sure that the weaker colour provides the field and the stronger colour is used sparingly to create the contrast. It is the red dots of the poppies seen against the field or background of green that make such a happy contrast. Dots of green on a field of red, on the other hand, would contrast badly.

In using harmonious colours—those that are close together in the spectrum—many gardeners draw an imaginary line between green and red on the colour wheel. This, in effect, gives two ranges of colour—the one principally made up of

LEFT: A strong and interesting contrast—tiny splashes of red (tulips) dotted here and there amongst green foliage and cream-coloured flowers (daffodils).

yellow, and the other principally of blue. By restricting yourself to one or the other of these two ranges, you will probably manage to avoid the pitfalls that undisciplined use of colour presents. Never forget the presence of green in the garden and the very important role it plays.

Colour is said to have three dimensions—hue, tone and saturation. Hue refers to the colour as it occurs in the spectrum. Tone refers to the intensity or brightness of a colour. We talk of light or dark tones. And saturation refers to the purity of colour. Hues are fully, or intensely, saturated but, as they are mixed more and more with light grey or white, their purity is progressively lessened and they are said to be washed out, or less saturated. Palest pink is the least saturated version of red (i.e. it is red containing the greatest amount of white) and lavender is the least saturated version of purple. The more intense the light the stronger and more saturated the colour needs to be to give a truly coloured effect. Whites and pastel colours look feeble during the daytime in subtropical and Mediterranean countries, whereas fully saturated colours hold their own. Towards dusk, however, the fully saturated colours appear to retreat, and the least saturated ones and whites come into glowing prominence.

By careful planting, you can have a garden that is yellow in spring, blue in summer and red in autumn, but to create the sort of effect that visitors will remember, the entire scheme must be convincing. To create such a garden, the colour of the trees, shrubs, hedges, and lawns, as well as the colour of the walls and buildings must be fully taken into account.

In a monochromatic scheme where, let's say, you are limiting yourself to yellow—and even giving 'yellow' the broadest interpretation by including dark cream and pale yellow-orange—you will find that the shapes and textures of leaves, flowers and shrubs stand out with clarity and harmony. This applies regardless of what single flower colour is used. One of the incidental advantages of using yellow is that there are so many flowers and shrubs with yellow variegated leaves that can, used imaginatively, add to the interest and excitement of the picture. In a polychromatic scheme, in which several flower colours are used, it is the colours alone that capture attention.

Gertrude Jekyll, the great English garden designer of the late Victorian era, was possibly the first to use monochromatic garden schemes. She did so, fully aware of the power of colour to affect the mood of the onlooker, and designed gardens in which the visitor passed through a hedge from an enclosure of blue flowers, which produced a cool and restful mood, to the warmth and brightness of a yellow garden. Such sudden changes of mood invariably provoked exclamations of delight.

Building on the ideas of Gertrude Jekyll and others, Vita Sackville-West at Sissinghurst in Kent, made single-colour gardens that have had a worldwide influence on garden design. One of the last enclosures that she designed at Sissinghurst was the White Garden, made shortly after the Second World War. White flowers and all the off-whites and creams are thrown into startling relief against the dark-green of the yew hedges. To ease the transition between dark green and white, she filled large areas of the White Garden with grey foliage and started a trend that continues to this day.

Vita Sackville-West would have agreed that, in general, white gardens are the easiest to make whereas red ones are probably the most difficult. Red flowers seen against a background of green foliage tend to retreat into the background and lose their vigour. It is a well known optical phenomenon that light colours advance towards the eye and dark colours retreat. Red flowers, however, can appear to be impelled forwards if placed in front of dusky purple and magenta backgrounds. Such a ploy was used in the red borders at Hidcote, in the Cotswolds, England, where red flowers were placed in front of purple-leaved plants such as the purple-leaf filbert (*Corylus maxima* 'Purpurea') and the dark red foliage of low-clipped Norway maples.

Colours affect different people in different ways. To make your garden a true reflection of your own personality, which will immediately give it an air of integrity, choose your favourite colour—or colours—and plan how to introduce it most effectively into your garden.

RIGHT: You can play interesting games with colour. The red azaleas seen against the blue field of bluebells present the eye with two strongly contrasting colours. Yet the white flowers (dogwoods and rhododendrons) capture the attention to such an extent that it almost becomes a case of red seen against a white field, and the red–blue contrast becomes less dominating.

DRAWING
UP YOUR
OWN PLANS

A Bird's-eye View

The aim of this chapter is to give ideas on how to draw up a rudimentary survey and plan. By measuring your garden and drawing its dimensions to scale on a piece of paper you will get a totally new view—and a very important one—of your garden.

The plan of a garden is the same as a bird's-eye view of it. Even though plans are two dimensional you can give the illusion of depth by delineating the more important objects, such as the house, with thicker and heavier lines. In fact, you can draw your plan as if it were an aerial view. Using watercolours or coloured pencils, paint the roof of the house as it actually looks from above, place a grey area on one side of each plant to show how the shadows might appear if seen from above, and paint the plants with the proportions they will attain at maturity.

LEFT: Having measured the outer dimensions of your house, measure the distances between the house and the outer boundaries. This will give you a sense of proportion and you will be able to begin a plan for the space you have in your garden.

PREVIOUS PAGE: A garden like this does not simply evolve; it is the direct result of careful planning. Although the basic framework is structured, established plants have softened the edges.

Do a simple survey of your garden before attempting to draw your plan. With a reasonably long tape-measure, measure the outer dimensions of your house, and note the position of all outside doors and windows on the ground floor. Mark these in on your plan. Then measure the distances between the house and the outer boundaries of the land. If your house occupies practically the full width of the land with very little space down either side, then do a separate survey of the front and the back, which are, in fact, two separate gardens. If you are unsure of any of your measurements, remeasure! Any mistakes in your survey will mean that your garden plans are not drawn true to scale. Now plot the position of all existing trees, paths, garden beds, lawns, sheds and walls.

Before committing your survey to paper you will need to decide on a scale and this will depend on whether you are working in metric or imperial measurements. For a small garden of 10 to 30 metres in length, the best metric scale to use is 1:100. This means that one centimetre in your drawing equals 100 centimetres (or 1 metre) of your survey measurement. The closest equivalent to this scale in imperial measurements is ($^1/_8$) inch = 1 foot. In an even smaller garden you might consider using the larger scale of 1:50 metric and, later on, when designing garden details such as flights of steps you will probably find 1:10 metric the easiest scale.

Now you are ready to put your survey on paper. You will need sheets of white paper, an HB and a 2H pencil, an eraser, a scale rule, a compass for large circles, a template for small circles, two clear plastic triangles (one with angles of 45°, 45°, 90° and the other with 30°, 60°, 90°) and several French curves to help you draw different sorts of wavy lines. You will also find it helpful to have a roll of thin tracing paper so that, when you reach the planning stage, you can experiment with different ideas without constantly having to restart the plan on white paper.

Using the completed survey and sheets of tracing paper torn from the roll, prepare a structural plan of the garden, which will show all the details of the proposed hard landscaping—that is, the paths, walls, terraces, swimming pool, garden shed etc. When you have completed the structural plan you may decide to do further drawings on a larger scale, for example a plan showing the stone terrace in great detail as you envisage it. This would be indispensable in showing how the stone mason should cut the paving slabs, and in what pattern they should be laid.

Your next task is to draw up your planting plan. This obviously has to relate to the structural plan, but structural details need only be outlined if you so wish. On the planting plan put a cross (x), with a number or letter beside it, to mark where a particular plant is to be positioned. In the margin, make a note of the name of the plant and

the number or letter assigned to it. The plan will be easier to understand if you use a circle or squiggly line, drawn to scale, to represent the outline of the plant at maturity. Existing plants to be retained in the scheme are usually denoted by a heavier and more pronounced circle than are proposed plants. You can distinguish between conifers

and deciduous trees either by using an indented and angular outline for conifers and a rounded one for deciduous trees, or by painting the conifers dark-green on your plan and deciduous trees light-green. Use cross-hatching to show groundcover plants, which are difficult to indicate since they are usually growing beneath other plants.

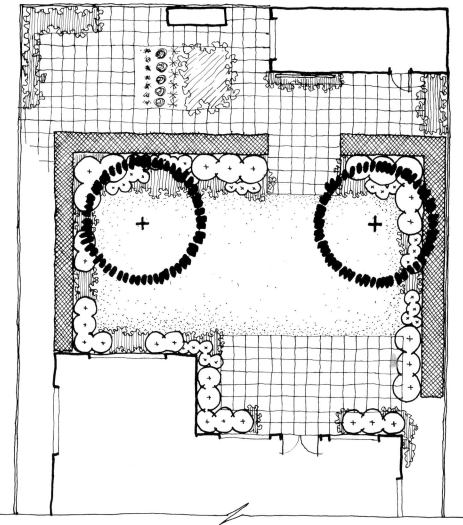

ABOVE: Measure the distance from the house to the outer boundaries of the land and draw up your plan as a scaled-down aerial view. Mark in existing trees, shrubs, flower beds, buildings and walls before plotting the positions for new plants and structures.

In designing this stone terrace, the dimensions of each of the rectangular stone slabs was decided on the drawing board.
Scaled plans are invaluable in precisely conveying your ideas to the builders and stonemasons.

GARDEN STYLES

The Formal Garden

The formal garden had its origins in the medieval monasteries and convents where the walled vegetable gardens were tended by the monks and nuns.

During the Renaissance, particularly in Italy and Holland, gardens of formal design underwent many refinements. Because the times were more politically stable, defensive walls were not so necessary and gardens were no longer confined behind them. Furthermore, powerful ruling families, rich prelates like Cardinal Ferdinand de Medici, and the more influential nobles were the great patrons of the garden at this time. No longer was a formal layout used because it was the most efficient answer to growing vegetables in a limited space, as was the case in the medieval monasteries and convents. Rather, it was used because it could be highly decorative, imparting an air of tremendous grandeur which the owners found flattering.

OPPOSITE: This small but famous private garden of landscape designer Thomas Church in San Francisco has a formal ground plan and a relaxed planting scheme of roses, hydrangeas and geraniums.

PREVIOUS PAGE: The pleasing symmetry of a formal garden at Linden Hall in England is apparent in this view of the garden. Carefully clipped hedges and topiary against a backdrop of herbaceous borders.

Instead of defensive stone walls at the perimeter there were likely to be hedges and rows of trees. Water was introduced to the garden for its emotive qualities. In many gardens such as the Villa Lante near Rome, which still exists today, water became the focal point. From the grotto at the highest level, the water descends a slope, finally reaching a large square pool at the lowest level. Fountains and cascades, too, were used to great effect in Italian Renaissance gardens. And there were parterres (or formal arrangements) of clipped box hedges.

During the seventeenth century when the formal garden reached its climax, the most innovative and brilliant gardens were being made in France, the most distinguished of which, such as Vaux-le-Vicomte and Versailles, were designed by André le Nôtre. Today formal gardens are experiencing a strong revival, but are fitting into smaller spaces. The dimensions of parterres in many instances are less than those of the rooms of a house. And some knot gardens are even smaller.

In making a formal garden it is advisable in most instances not to place it in an open space. It is important to isolate a formal garden from surroundings with which it has nothing in common and this can best be done by enclosing it. Frame it with a wall or a hedge as you would frame a picture.

Many different kinds of hedging plant can be used for a perimeter hedge, the optimum height of which is probably two metres—that is, of sufficient height to visually contain the garden but allowing long distance views of the surroundings. Yew is the traditional choice because of its longevity and because it is evergreen and very dark green in colour, making it an excellent foil for other plants. Yew, however, does not thrive in all climates and other plants, such as bay laurel (*Laurus nobilis*), pittosporum (*Pittosporum tobira*), or escallonia might be considered. On the other hand, a brick or stone wall covered with climbing plants can be an equally happy solution.

Just as yew is the traditional plant to hedge the perimeter, so box is the plant most often used for the low hedges that enclose the garden beds of the parterre itself. The plant known as edging box (*Buxus sempervirens* 'Suffruticosa') is the species most commonly used for this purpose. The small leafed box (*Buxus microphylla*) is another good dwarf hedging plant.

Proportions are crucial in the making of a formal garden. The dimensions of the paths must not only be related to the dimensions of the garden beds, but must also allow people to move around the garden with comparative ease. It is essential to draw up plans, however simple, before embarking upon the construction of a formal garden.

The Formal Garden

*H*ere a solid brick wall in a small backyard garden provides the necessary framework for, and the excuse to create, a simple formal garden. Hedges of clipped box make a formal parterre, the focal point of which is a simple pool with waterlilies. This garden is, more than anything else, a collection of shrub roses. It could, however, be a collection of any type of shrub you wish, for example, viburnums or hydrangeas.

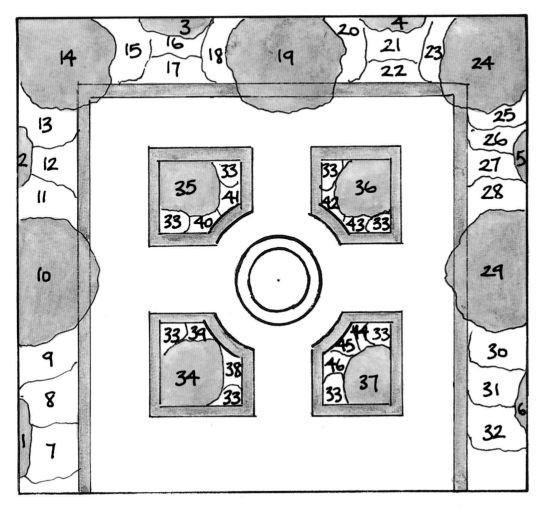

24. *Rosa* 'Frau Karl Druschki' height 1.5m (5ft)
25. *Echinops ritro* 'Veitch's Blue' (globe thistle) height to 1m (3ft)
26. *Convolvulus cneorum* (silver bush) height to 45cm (18in)
27. *Paeonia* 'Duchesse de Nemeurs' (peony) height 1m (3ft)
28. *Salvia nemorosa* 'May Night' (sage) height 1m (3ft)
29. *Rosa* 'Buff Beauty' height 1.5 m (5ft)
30. *Sedum spectabilis* (showy stonecrop) height 45cm (18in)
31. *Romneya coulteri* (tree poppy) height to 2.5m (8ft)
32. *Iris* x *germanica* (bearded iris) height 45cm (18in)
33. *Rosa* 'Iceberg' (plant eight; two in each central bed) height 1.5m (5ft)
34. *Rosa* 'Stanwell Perpetual' height 1.5m (5ft)
35. *Rosa* 'Constance Spry' height 1.5m (5ft)
36. *Rosa* 'Fantin Latour' height 1.5m (5ft)
37. *Rosa* 'Koenigin von Danemark' height 1.5m (5ft)
38. *Hosta plantaginea* (plantain lily) height 60cm (2ft)
39. *Myostis scorpioides* 'Mermaid' height 45cm (18in)
40. *Brunnera macrophylla* (Siberian bugloss) height 45cm (18in)
41. *Stachys byzantina* (lamb's ears) height 50cm (20in)
42. *Dianthus* 'Musgrave Pink' height 30cm (12in)
43. *Alchemilla mollis* (lady's mantle) height 45cm (18in)
44. *Geranium endressii* (cranesbill) height 50cm (20in)
45. *Lamium maculatum* (dead nettle) height 30cm (1ft)
46. *Nepeta* x *faassenii* (catmint) height 30cm (1ft)

Key to planting scheme

1. *Rosa* 'Gloire de Dijon' climber
2. *Rosa* 'Mermaid' vigorous climber
3. *Rosa* 'New Dawn' vigorous climber
4. *Rosa* 'Albertine' climber
5. *Rosa* 'Mme Alfred Carrière' climber
6. *Rosa* 'Albéric Barbier' vigorous climber
7. *Paeonia* 'Sarah Bernhardt' (peony) height 1m (3ft)
8. *Centranthus ruber* height to 1m (3ft)
9. *Salvia turkestanica* (sage) height 1 m (3ft)
10. *Rosa* 'Penelope' height 1.5m (5ft)
11. *Veronica longifolia* height 1m (3ft)
12. *Helleborus orientalis* (lenten rose) height 45cm (18in)
13. *Anemone x hybrida* 'Honorine Jobert' (windflower) height 75cm (30in)
14. *Rosa* 'Pax' height 1.5m (5ft)
15. *Santolina chamaecyparissus* (lavender cotton) height to 60cm (2ft)
16. *Delphinium* 'Blue Nile' (larkspur) height 1.2m (4ft)
17. *Lilium regale* (regal lily) height to 1.5m (5ft)
18. *Nicotiana* (flowering tobacco) height 45cm (18in)
19. *Rosa* 'Nevada' height 1.5m (5ft)
20. *Nicotiana* (flowering tobacco) height 45cm (18in)
21. *Delphinium* 'Loch Leven' height 1.2m (4ft)
22. *Lilium regale* (regal lily) height 1.5m (5ft)
23. *Anemone x hybrida* 'Honorine Jobert' (windflower) height 60cm (2ft)

The Wild Garden

The wild garden can almost be looked upon as a state of mind. What appears wild to one person might seem almost manicured to another. The important thing is not to feel constrained by tradition when making a wild garden.

Wild gardens can be made anywhere from small backyards in New York to the outback in Australia. Climate and space do not present drawbacks. The best ones, however, have some unifying factor that, although perhaps contrasting paradoxically with the spirit that inspired the garden in the first place, holds the composition together and makes it satisfying to both the eye and the spirit.

One of the obvious advantages of the wild garden is that it can be devised to be low maintenance. Do not assume, however, that just because it is wild it is low maintenance. There may be a lawn, or part of a lawn, that needs to be regularly mown. Some of the trees and shrubs may

LEFT: Twenty years ago, this garden in suburban Detroit was farmland. Rusting farm machinery left behind by the farmers is now surreal sculpture in a garden that strongly evokes the spirit of the American prairies. The growing of wild flowers and unmown grass is becoming increasingly popular all over the world.

require regular pruning. And a surrounding hedge—which lends a 'wilder' feeling to the garden than a wall or fence would—will have to be clipped every once in a while. There are two good reasons for making a wild garden; firstly, it can create an air of limitless space and, secondly, it can add a sense of mystery to the scene.

The wild garden in a temperate climate presents a splendid opportunity to plant sheets of bulbs beneath the trees and in particular, amongst the long grass. The crocuses, snowdrops, daffodils and bluebells will appear early in the season while the grass is still short after winter. When the bulbs have finished flowering the grass will grow long, summer wild flowers will appear and there will be no need to lift the bulbs. Their dying leaves will be hidden by the long grass, and will magically appear once again the following spring.

A small inner city house with a terrace or patio close to the house for enjoying the outdoors during the warmer months could have in its small backyard a nearly impenetrable forest of bamboo plants overhung by a few large trees with tall slender trunks. A wide gravel path might wander tantalisingly around a clump of bamboo and then disappear from sight. Lighting the garden at night would add a further air of mystery. By blocking out

The Wild Garden

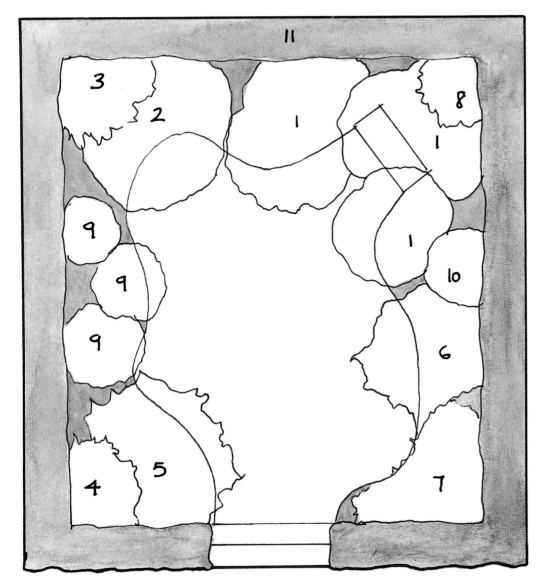

Key to planting scheme

1. *Magnolia hypoleuca* (plant three) height to 6m (20ft)
2. *Koelreuteria paniculata* (golden rain tree) height to 6m (20ft)
3. *Buddleia madagascariensis* height to 5m (16ft)
4. *Buddleia alternifolia* (fountain buddleia) height to 3m (10ft)
5. *Paulownia tomentosa* (mountain jacaranda; princess tree) height to 9m (30ft)
6. *Cornus nuttallii* (mountain dogwood) height to 5m (16ft)
7. *Phyllostachys nigra* var. *henonsis*
8. *Hydrangea aspera* height to 1.2m (4ft)
9. *Callistemon pallidus* (bottlebrush) (plant three) height 2m (6ft)
10. *Itea ilicifolia* (hollyleaf sweetspire) height to 1.5m (5ft)
11. *Buxus sempervirens* (common box) height to 1m (3ft)

*A*t the back of a house is a terrace of crazy paving partially enclosed by a loosely clipped hedge. A gap at the centre gives a tantalising view down a long vista into a wild garden. The wildness of this garden is enhanced by contrasting the mown lawn with the long natural grass. By keeping the hedge only roughly clipped and by losing the boundary in shadow and hiding it behind trees and shrubs, an illusion of almost infinite space is created.

much of the view of the city and disguising the perimeter fence, such a garden gives a tremendous sense of space, even though several skyscrapers might be plainly visible above the trees.

Another sort of small wild garden can be created by planting the perimeter with a loosely clipped billowing hedge that surrounds the entire 'wild' area, apart from a comparatively narrow entrance leading from a terrace immediately behind the house. Because only parts of the 'wild' garden would be seen from the terrace or the ground floor of the house at any one time, a sense of greater space and of mystery would be created. Allowing the grass around the perimeter of the garden to grow tall and rank beneath a dense canopy of trees, and planting it with spring-flowering bulbs would invoke a feeling of controlled wilderness.

A wild garden should appear forsaken but not forlorn!

ABOVE: This garden, evoking a wild atmosphere, is composed of sheets of perennials, such as iris, astilbe and hostas, which merge with the trees beyond.

RIGHT: A natural rock and indigenous forest tree are the starting point for this simple and apt woodland garden of alpine flora, spring bulbs and azaleas.

The Cottage Garden

The term 'cottage garden' immediately conjures up romantic visions of small gardens close by the great seafaring ports of the eighteenth and nineteenth centuries. Extraordinary treasures in the form of cuttings and seeds were borne home as gifts by husbands, sons and friends on sailing ships returning from little known corners of the world.

Whereas almost every type of garden is subject to the rules of unity, scale and harmony of colour, the cottage garden is so refreshingly free of most forms of constraint that it could almost be considered the odd one out amongst gardens. As the purpose of the cottage garden is to provide enjoyment and immediate gratification to the gardener, and as it rarely follows any but the most rudimentary plan, it is usually a delightfully spontaneous and unpredictable jumble of colour and types of plant. Many of the plants will have been acquired as cutting and seeds, from numerous interesting sources, just as in the sailing ship days.

The desire to create a cottage garden lies deep in most true gardeners. Even in the grandest and most formal of gardens you will usually find a cottage garden tucked away in some corner. Often these hidden cottage gardens serve as proving grounds where newly acquired plants, cuttings and seeds being considered for inclusion in the main part of the garden, either survive or perish. In other instances it is simply where the gardener indulges in the joy of unrestrainedly mixing together perennials, annuals and vegetables without following a rigid plan.

The front gardens of many suburban houses face the street and, lacking privacy, are not very conducive to quiet enjoyment. As a result, many people very wisely turn these spaces into cottage gardens. All sense of plant association and ecological compatibility is cast to the wind and you find divergent and surprising combinations such as roses, hibiscus shrubs and azaleas all growing together in chaotic splendour.

Spontaneity, the greatest strength of the cottage garden, is also perhaps its greatest weakness. While the collection of plants may look splendid during the summer months—a time when it is difficult for almost any garden not to look good—the cottage garden, because its composition usually lacks 'bones' to hold it together, may look forlorn and bedraggled during the winter. This can be overcome, however, by providing a backbone of evergreen shrubs throughout the beds and borders.

LEFT: Deep green is broken by the deep pink rose blooms in this wall of foliage. Roses are an essential ingredient of the successful cottage garden.

ABOVE: *The front door is a focal point in any garden and this one is particularly attractive with a mass of roses and a mass of mixed annual and perennial flowers in low beds.*

RIGHT: *Here is a true cottage garden in which larkspur, nicotiana and lilies provide an intoxicating mixture. Perennials that carry flowers in tall spikes are often the hallmark of the cottage garden landscape.*

The Cottage Garden

*T*he gate leading from the street into this garden can be seen behind the tree on the right-hand side. On entering the garden you walk under a small pergola covered in climbing roses which also clamber over the wooden fence. Each of the two garden beds is designed roughly in the shape of a cross, the crosses being formed by paving stones along which you can walk to see the plants or to maintain the beds. The two trees have been placed to give vertical relief to the predominantly horizontal scheme, although certain plants in the beds, such as the humea in the background will become quite large by the end of summer. It is important that the walls be covered with climbing plants, in this case climbing roses since the theme of the garden is roses.

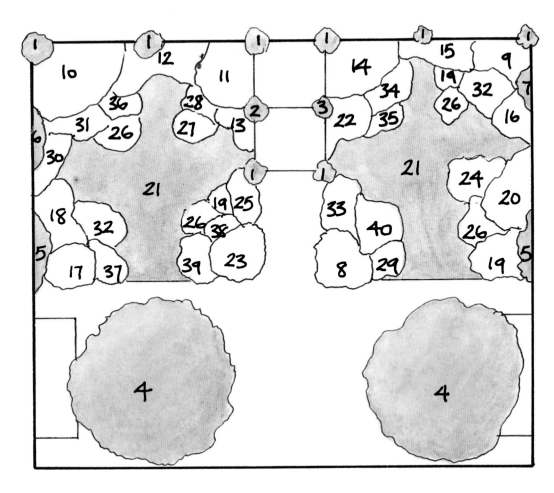

Key to planting scheme

1. *Rosa* 'Climbing Lady Hillingdon' climbing to 4m (13 ft)

2. *Clematis montana rubens* (anemone clematis) climbing to 5m (16ft)

3. *Clematis* 'The President' climbing to 4m (13ft)

4. *Malus baccata* var. *Mandschurica* (crab apple) height to 4m (13ft)

5. *Hydrangea petiolaris* (climbing hydrangea) climbing to 3m (10ft)

6. *Lonicera periclymenum* 'Graham Thomas' (honeysuckle) climbing to 3.5m (12ft)

7. *Passiflora caerulea* (blue passion flower) climbing to 3m (10ft)

8. *Hosta sieboldiana* (plantain lily) height to to 60cm (2ft)

9. *Digitalis purpurea* (foxglove) height 1.5m (5ft)

10. *Humea elegans* (incense plant) height 2m (6ft)

11. *Salvia sclarea* var. *Turkestanica* height to 1.4m (4ft)

12. *Mattholia* 'Giant Excelsior' (stock) height to 60cm (2ft)

13. *Lavandula angustifolia* 'Hidcote' (English lavender) height 1.2m (4ft)

14. *Verbascum* 'Gainsborough' (lambs' tails; mullein) height to 1.2m (4ft)

15. *Anchusa azurea* 'London Royalist' (alkanet) height to 1.5m (5ft)

16. *Thalictrum lucidum* (meadow rue) height height to 1.2m (4ft)

17. *Thymus vulgaris* (thyme) spreading to 5cm (2in)

18. *Rosmarinus officinalis* (common rosemary) height to 1.2 m (4ft)

19. *Viola Crystal Bowl* series (viola) (plant three) height 15cm (6in)

20. *Veronica austriaca teucrium* (speedwell)

21. *Viola calcarata* (as a carpet around all the stepping stones) height 5cm (2in)

22. *Lysimachia clethroides* (moneywort) height to 1m (3ft)

23. *Hebe cuppressoides* 'Boughton Dome' (veronica) height to 60cm (2ft)

24. *Iris x germanica* (flag iris) height to 45cm (18in)

25. *Euphorbia marginata* (snow-on-the-mountain; ghostweed)

26. *Nicotiana domino* (tobacco plant) (plant four) height to 45cm (18in)

27. *Pulmonaria saccharata* (lungwort) height 30cm (1ft)

28. *Eryngium oliverianum* (sea holly) height 60cm (2ft)

29. *Salvia patens* (sage) height 60cm (2ft)

30. *Amsonia tabernaemontana* height 60cm (2ft)

31. *Scabiosa caucasica* (pincushion flower) height to 45cm (18in)

32. *Rosa* 'Iceberg (plant two) height to 1.5m (5ft)

33. *Geranium wallichianum* 'Buxton's Blue' height to 30cm (1ft)

34. *Veronica longifolia* 'Romily Purple' (speedwell) height to 1m (3ft)

35. *Stokesia laevis* (stoke's aster) height to 45cm (18in)

36. *Phyllostachys suworowii*

37. *Salvia splendens* 'Cleopatra' (bonfire salvia) height to 45cm (18in)

38. *Veronica gentianoides* (speedwell) height to 45cm (18in)

39. *Geranium x magnificum* height to 50cm (20in)

40. *Acanthus spinosus* (mountain thistle) height to 1m (3ft)

The Small Backyard Garden

Having moved into a brand new house, what are you to do with a small backyard garden in which nothing yet exists? For instance, you may be faced with a level site of bare earth, a timber perimeter fence and a view of neighbouring roofs and electricity lines.

In Chapter 1 it was suggested that you draw up a list of the functions you wish your garden to serve, numbering them in order of priority. Having decided how you are going to make use of your available space, turn your attention to the view beyond the garden fence. Perhaps it is a view of distant mountains, the sea or a very attractive tree in a nearby garden. Select those things that you like and 'borrow' them for your own garden, but avoid planting trees that will eventually obscure them. Remember that you can add immeasurably to the charm of a distant or near object by framing it between trees or enabling it to be seen beneath the canopy of a tall tree.

LEFT: A small space can still include a seating arrangement, and a decorative element such as the birdbath provides a focus. An exotic effect has been created by plantings of bamboo, ferns and creeping ivy.

Now consider how you can hide the unattractive features of your view, such as neighbouring roofs or power lines, which detract from the calm and restful air you wish to create. The best way to hide the power lines is to disguise them with a small clump of trees that mimic the tone of their aluminium pylons. Such a choice of tree might be a group of birches in a cold snowy climate, or a species of silvery white-trunked eucalypt such as the lemon-scented gum (*Eucalyptus citriodora*) in a warmer climate. Be careful to choose eucalypts that will not eventually grow too tall, and plant them well away from the foundations of the buildings.

You can probably manage to hide the roof next door by planting a medium-sized tree. Deciduous trees which, in general, grow faster than conifers, are a good choice in a cold climate as you will not be using the garden very much during the winter months when the trees are leafless. In a warmer climate, however, you may actually use the garden more in winter than in summer and so an evergreen— not necessarily a conifer—will be more suitable. In warmer climates some evergreens such as eucalypts are amongst the fastest growing trees. Ask local nurseries for their advice and then, in the nearest botanic gardens or public park where the plants are labelled, look at mature specimens of the trees suggested. Borrow specialist books on trees from the local library. Your choice of tree is absolutely critical to the future success of your garden and you would do well to consider all the possibilities carefully.

Try and hide the garden fence as much as possible with shrubs and climbing plants. This, curiously enough, gives an illusion of greater space since, if the fence is lost in shadow and you cannot actually see it, the shadowy area appears boundless. Good climbing plants to use in a temperate climate are *Hydrangea petiolaris,* as it will eventually end up looking more like a huge shrub than a climber, and *Wisteria sinensis*. Both these plants, however, lose their leaves in winter. *Wisteria sinensis* is also a good choice in a subtropical climate. An ideal evergreen climbing plant for a warm climate is star jasmine (*Trachelospermum jasminoides*) which will likewise eventually give total cover.

Avoid overplanting in the small garden; it is the most common error in gardening. Establish the mature height and span of each tree and shrub, and ensure that sufficient space is left for healthy growth. While overlapping of branches and foliage is acceptable, even desirable, overcrowding results in certain species failing to thrive, and eventually requiring removal.

RIGHT: A small white seat at the end of a path creates the illusion of greater depth. Flowering perennials and shrubs have been allowed to cascade onto the path, breaking up the solid appearance of the paving.

The Small Backyard Garden

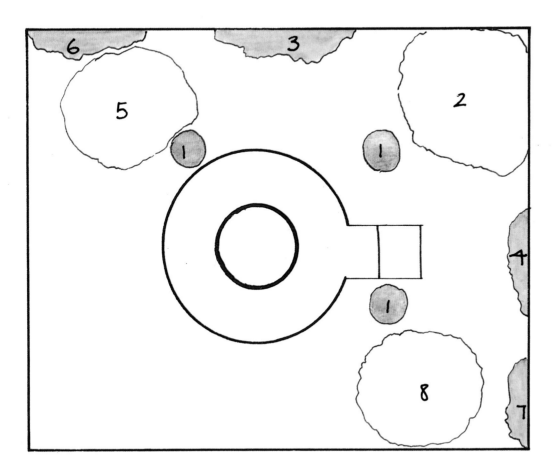

Key to planting scheme

1. *Eucalyptus citriodora* (lemon-scented gum) height 15m (50ft)
2. *Callistemon citrinus* 'Splendens' (crimson bottlebrush) height 5m (16ft)
3. *Trachelospermum jasminoides* (star jasmine) climbing to 5m (16ft)
4. *Plumbago auriculata* (leadwort) climbing to 4m (13ft)
5. *Camellia reticulata* height 7.5m (25ft), spread 4m (12ft)
6. *Wisteria floribunda* 'Alba' climbing to 6m (20ft)
7. *Hardenbergia comptoniana* (sarsaparilla) climbing to 4m (13ft)
8. *Osmanthus x burkwoodii* height 3m (10ft), spread 3 m (10ft)

What are you to do if faced with a wooden-fenced, bare-earth space? In a warm climate, one answer is to plant quick-growing trees that within a few years will provide shade and hide surrounding buildings. The trees provide vertical accents where so much is horizontal. Consider concealing the fence. There are two principal ways this can be done—by growing climbing plants that will all but cover the fence or by placing shrubs in front of the fence to give it a three-dimensional covering. A barbecue has been placed in close proximity to the table and chair for outdoor entertaining. The lawn provides a space for children to play.

The Low Maintenance Garden

Low maintenance gardens are for those people who have little time for gardening or limited space.

LAWNS

When considering a low maintenance garden, first ask yourself whether you want a lawn or not. Lawns require regular mowing and, from time to time, need to be fertilised and aerated. Furthermore, finding space to store the lawnmower in an inner city garden may pose a considerable problem. Perhaps you will decide in favour of a lawn because you can afford to pay a professional to maintain the grass and to cut it every few days during the summer. However, if you yourself are the person who will have to mow and maintain the lawn, you may very well decide to do without one.

If you do decide on this course of action, what are you to do with the space that might otherwise have been a lawn? One solution is to pave it with either stone, bricks or tiles, but paving, properly done, not only involves considerable expense, it also involves placing a mineral surface where there might otherwise have been plant life. To compensate for this

ABOVE: The strength of this garden lies in its contrasts of texture and form. The timber decking needs only occasional sweeping and the plants, in particular the tree-ferns and impatiens ('Busy Lizzy'), require little attention.

OPPOSITE: A low maintenance garden constructed almost entirely of brickwork is softened by climbing plants that smother the walls, shrubs that cascade over the edges of the planter boxes and flowers growing from small terracotta pots.

hard surface you could soften the appearance of your garden by covering the fence or garden wall with climbing plants. Instead of paving, however, you might consider laying gravel, although weeds sometimes present a problem by thriving in gravel. Another solution, particularly in a small garden or on a sloping site, is to build a wooden deck.

GARDEN BEDS

The next thing to consider is the maintenance of the garden beds. You may decide not to have garden beds at all, but without these you can hardly say you have a garden. Instead of taking this radical step, you might consider planting low maintenance shrubs and perennials.

LOW MAINTENANCE SHRUBS

Low maintenance shrubs are those that require little or no pruning, that are not subject to pests and diseases and therefore need little or no spraying, and that do not need dead-heading after flowering. Most regrettably this immediately eliminates roses. Most camellias, azaleas and rhododendrons, however, can survive with little maintenance although, it must be said, they give of their best if they receive more attention. Avoid shrubs that require pruning after flowering.

LOW MAINTENANCE PERENNIALS

These are those flowers that do not have to be dug up and divided every second year, and that do not suffer from mildew and other diseases. Like all plants, every perennial will differ according to climate and locality and so it is best to check with your local nurseries as to which are the best for your area. This should not, however, prevent you from experimenting and trying to extend the range of plants in your garden beyond those which the local nurseries offer.

WEEDS

The final consideration is weeds. Weeding is a time-consuming job. The answer is to use groundcover plants that compete so strongly with weeds that they shade them out of existence. There are many groundcover plants capable of this, but one, the bugle plant (*Ajuga reptans*) is worth mentioning. The bugle plant succeeds, by means of runners, in creating a nearly impenetrable carpet of tight foliage. It produces attractive blue flowers in spring and early summer and is one of those rare plants capable of thriving across a broad spectrum of climatic zones. Until groundcovering plants spread and become established, a thick mulch layer will certainly help to prevent unwanted weed growth. Use an organic mulch, such as well-rotted compost, manure or leaf litter, and the plants will gradually benefit from additional nutrients while weeds are simultaneously suppressed.

RIGHT: This small front garden contains an eclectic collection of plants such as rosemary, tobacco, Ruta graveolens *and variegated sage, planted in the gaps between the low maintenance brick paving to prevent weeds taking hold.*

The Low Maintenance Garden

*C*obbled paving, brick walls and raised masonry planter boxes all help to reduce maintenance to a minimum. Choosing shrubs that do not need dead-heading or pruning after flowering also helps. Plants such as bamboo, if contained within planting boxes and not allowed to spread, are low maintenance plants. The use of extensive groundcover plants in any garden bed normally keeps weeds to a minimum. It is important that a subdued colour scheme harmonise with the contrasting foliage.

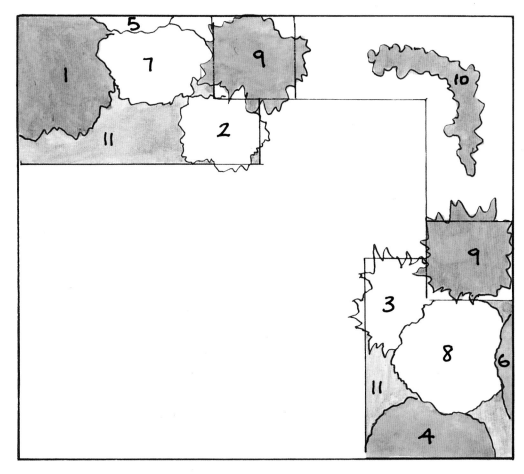

Key to planting scheme

1. *Acer japonicum* 'Aconitifolium' (Japanese maple) height 5m (16ft), spread 5m (15ft)

2. *Viburnum davidii* height 2.5m (8ft)

3. *Hosta sieboldiana* (plantain lily) height to 1m (3ft)

4. *Magnolia x wieseneri* height 5m (16ft), spread 5m (16ft)

5. *Hedera colchica* 'Sulphur Heart' (ivy) climbing to 5m (16ft)

6. *Hydrangea petiolaris* (climbing hydrangea) climbing to 3m (10ft)

7. *Hydrangea quercifolia* (oak-leaf hydrangea) height 2m (6ft), spread 1.5m (5ft)

8. *Viburnum x pragense* height 2.5m (8ft), spread 1.5m (5ft)

9. *Pseudosasa japonica* height 1.5m (4.5ft), spread 1m (3ft)

10. Waterlilies planted in submerged pots

11. A mixture of:

 (a) *Pulmonaria angustifolia* (lungwort) height 30cm (1ft)

 (b) *Vinca minor* (lesser periwinkle) height 60cm (2ft)

 (c) *Lamium orvala* (giant dead nettle) height 60cm (2ft)

 (d) *Epimedium grandiflorum* (barrenwort) height 30cm (1ft)

 (e) *Convallaria majalis* (lily-of-the-valley) height 20cm (8in)

The Desert Garden

Dramatic effects can be created by making a desert garden using cactus plants and succulents. Cacti are themselves considered succulents, a word derived from the Latin *succos*, meaning juice. Having the ability to store water in their swollen leaves, stems and roots, these plants can survive long droughts. The vast majority of succulents are natives of desert regions, but there are a few interesting exceptions. Some succulents come from the tropical jungles of Central and South America, others from the cold, alpine regions of Europe and others still, from the shorelines of saltwater lakes and oceans.

Only attempt to make a desert garden if you are living in a hot, dry climate. Most succulents look out of place under dark, grey rainy skies, and many will not tolerate moist conditions. To set the scene it helps—although it is by no means necessary—to have the garden enclosed by stone walls, or walls rendered in the adobe fashion. A rock garden containing succulent plants and placed in the centre of a bright green lawn looks incongruous.

Succulents will grow in any reasonably light, well drained soil. The three basic needs of these plants are good aeration, steady nourishment and perfect drainage. Plant your succulents in a soil mix formed of equal parts of sand, soil and leaf mould. Use only clean, coarse

ABOVE: Here the designer has stuck rigidly to the theme of a desert garden, producing a garden that is both simple and extremely effective.

OPPOSITE: The brilliant simplicity of this sculptor's garden is achieved by using desert colours on the walls and floor, and by exercising the strictest discipline in the choice of plants. The result is one of striking unity.

river sand; fine beach sand packs hard and may contain salt or other impurities. Leaf mould should be well rotted and preferably from hardwood trees such as oak. Any good garden loam will do for the soil. These ingredients should be well mixed and coarsely screened to make a loose, friable, sweet-smelling compost.

Desert plants tend to look most natural in a free-form bed in which rocks and plants are carefully arranged to simulate a tiny desert landscape. Such a bed may be as small as one metre deep by two metres long. On the other hand, the entire garden can be made into a desert landscape. You might take advantage of a natural slope in the garden or, on a level site, you could create a mound or a tiny hill on which to plant succulents. Desert plants have a very strong individual character of their own and so it is important that your beds of succulents harmonise with the rest of your garden.

Although succulents do not like any but the lightest shade, it is important to use shade to create relief and interest. Water, surrounded by desert palms such as *Washingtonia robusta*, the shade of which is not too dense for succulents, can be used to create an oasis.

RIGHT AND OPPOSITE: The shape and texture of these desert plants are strangely reminiscent of the paintings of American painter Georgia O'Keefe who lived in the desert of New Mexico. They are strongly architectural and present the gardener with lots of potentially interesting contrasts when designing a desert garden.

The Desert Garden

Key to planting scheme

1 & 2. *Epiphyllum* (orchid cactus) height 60cm (2ft)

3. *Ferocactus wislizenii* height 1m (3ft)

4. *Cereus jamacaru* or *Cereus nobilis* (torch thistle) height to 2m (6ft)

5. *Opuntia monacantha* (Indian fig) height to 2m (6ft)

6. *Echinocactus grusonii* (barrel cactus) height 75cm (30in)

7. *Cercidium floridum*

9. *Aloe ferox* height 45cm (18in)

9. *Sedum rubrotinctum* (stonecrop) height to 30cm (1ft)

10. *Echeveria glauca* (Mexican snowball) height 30cm (1ft)

11. *Crassula socialis* (jade plant) height to 30cm (1ft)

12. *Aeonium canariense* (Canary island rose)

*T*he mood of this desert garden is enhanced by having a rough field-stone wall as a background and by having large stones in the garden bed amongst the plants. Desert gardens using cactus plants and succulents are liable to look desolate if there is no shade. The tree in the foreground is chosen because it, too, is a desert species and casts a very light shade through which the desert plants can be seen in sunlight.

The Subtropical Garden

The wonderful thing about subtropical plants is that they enable you to create bold and lush effects using a comparatively small number of different species.

With one type of palm tree, one clump of bamboo, a single species of philodendron, a few banana trees, one variety of hibiscus and a datura tree, the skeletal outline of a small 'jungle' garden can be made. It is in the exotic contrasts of such things as the hanging fronds of the palm, the huge fleshy leaves of the banana, the arching canes and busy pattern of the leaves of the bamboo and the heavily scented hanging trumpet flowers of the datura that a subtropical paradise garden can be made.

The secret in creating any type of garden is unity. Everything that you do in the garden should be a positive step towards fulfilling your basic theme. Anything that goes against the character you have chosen for your garden will

RIGHT: The hanging palm trees create a romantic effect. The foliage of subtropical plants is thrown into pleasing relief against the background of white walls.

OPPOSITE: The lushness of subtropical foliage enables a dense screen to be created in a relatively narrow space. Palms with a variety of frond colours, shapes and textures blend with other foliage plants.

create a sense of incongruity. For example, placing a bed of roses, or even a single rose bush, anywhere in a 'jungle' garden will destroy the magic and harmony of the subtropical plants and the subtropical plants will, in the same way, destroy the harmony of the roses. The eye becomes confused by this juxtaposition of inappropriate plant types.

Keep the planting as simple as possible and mass the same elements together, for example a large clump of *Strelitzia nicolae* with its upright, dark green foliage makes an interesting contrast to the lighter green, hanging foliage of Abyssinian banana (*Musa ensete*).

One of the aims when planting a subtropical garden is to create a sense of visual cool. Choose plants with dark green foliage—a cool colour in itself—and plant them so that they hang over paths and terraces to provide shade and so create a further feeling of cool.

A subtropical garden will not thrive in any but a subtropical climate. In colder regions the garden may be created in a large greenhouse or conservatory. For those living in desert or Mediterranean climates, however, one possibility is to create either a desert or a Mediterranean garden in the main part of the garden, and to plant a subtropical paradise garden in a courtyard, either in the centre of the house or at the side. Provided the subtropical garden is contained within a wall or hedge, which serves to emphasise its distinctness from the rest of the garden, no disharmony or confusion should result.

RIGHT: Palm trees and lush ferns set amidst pebbles beside the swimming pool in this garden have been designed to re-create the tropical feeling of the grounds of a famous Hawaiian hotel.

The Subtropical Garden

Key to planting scheme

1. *Musa* 'Lady's Finger' (banana) (plant three) height 3m (10ft)
2. *Cycas revoluta* (sago palm) height 2m (6ft)
3. *Datura suaveolens* (angel's trumpet) height 1.2m (4ft)
4. *Gardenia* 'Professor Pucci' (giant gardenia) height 1m (3ft)
5. *Hibiscus rosa-sinensis* (rose of China) height 2.5m (8ft)
6. *Philodendron selloum* height 2m (6ft)
7. *Alpinia nutans* (ginger) height 1.5m (5ft)
8. *Alocasia macrorrhiza* (spoon lily) height 1.5m (5ft)
9. *Monstera deliciosa* (fruit salad plant) height 3m (10ft)
10. *Clivia miniata* (kaffir lily) (plant 15) height 60cm (2ft)
11. *Hymenocallis x macrostephana* (plant ten) height 45cm (18in)
12. *Gardenia radicans* (plant nine) height 90cm (3ft)
13. *Strelitzia reginae* (bird-of-paradise flower) (plant seven) height 1.5m (4ft)
14. *Crinum yemense* (plant 12) height 1m (3ft)
15. *Plectranthus oertendahlii* (prostrate coleus; Brazilian coleus) (plant 12) height 30cm (1ft)
16. *Ophiopogon japonicus* (mondo grass) (plant 25) height 45cm (18in)
17. *Soleirolia soleirolii* (plant 30)
18. *Jasminum azoricum* climbing to 3m (10ft)
19. *Mandevilla laxa* (Chilean jasmine) climbing to 2.5m (8ft)
20. *Mucuna sempervirens*
21. *Mandevilla x amablis* 'Alice du Pont' climbing to 3m (10 ft)
22. *Thunbergia grandiflora* (Bengal clock vine) climbing to 3m (10ft)
23. *Arecastrum* (queen palm) can grow to 12m (40ft)

*S*ubtropical plants become even more exotic when seen in proximity to water. This means that lush and verdant effects can be made by creating a jungle of foliage with plants such as palms, banana trees and philodendrons around a swimming pool. The more successful you are at hiding the perimeter fence, and any non-subtropical surroundings, the greater the unity.

The Mediterranean Garden

The criterion used by many people of what constitutes a 'Mediterranean' region is whether the orange tree thrives there. Roughly speaking, such areas have hot, dry summers and mild, moist winters. In addition to regions bordering the Mediterranean Sea, the following regions have true Mediterranean climates—central and southern California, parts of southern and western Australia, South Africa's western Cape Province, the Canary Islands and part of the coast of Chile. In addition, eastern Australia, the south and south-western regions of the British Isles, south-west Europe, the southern United States, southern Japan and the North Island of New Zealand provide conditions conducive to the cultivation of Mediterranean plants.

LEFT: A Mediterranean mood has been invoked by the elements of this garden including the paving, the planting and the colour of the walls. The important thing about this Mediterranean-style courtyard is the discipline of its design.

In making a Mediterranean garden, the ultimate goal is to create a physically cool and visually refreshing environment in which to enjoy the climate, which is warm, if not actually hot, for much of the year.

In such climates, the terrace or courtyard closest to the house becomes an outdoor room—as important as any indoor room—in which to live and entertain. An outdoor table should ideally be placed beneath a pergola which provides total shade in summer and allows in the sun in winter. Perhaps the best covering for such a pergola is the grape vine because it is both deciduous and quick growing. To obtain edible grapes of good quality, however, it is necessary to spend time pruning, training and spraying the vine. This might be beyond the ambitions of many gardeners, in which case low maintenance ornamental grape vines provide an ideal compromise. In any event, it is advisable to see a local nursery for varieties best suited to your area. Instead of grape vines, deciduous climbing plants such as wisteria or climbing roses, both of which produce sweetly scented flowers instead of fruit, might be grown over the pergola. Or, use a mixture of climbing plants and add some evergreen ones such

as star jasmine (*Trachelospermum jasminoides*)

To create a sense of coolness beyond the pergola, a tree with dense green leaves could be grown to shade at least part of the terrace. Trees to consider are the Canary palm, *Phoenix canariensis*, the carob, *Ceratonia siliqua*, or the Japanese loquat, *Eriobotrya japonica*. It is possible to create Mediterranean gardens without using a single plant native to the Mediterranean region. Natives of Australia, California, South Africa and the Canary Islands can all be used and provide the gardener with a wide choice.

Garden beds can be incorporated as part of a terrace or, where space does not permit this, small trees like citrus or olives, shrubs like Californian lilac or rock roses, and flowers like pelargoniums can be grown in either terracotta or concrete pots. This creates a containerised garden.

In larger gardens, hedges, whether loosely or tightly clipped into shape, can be made from many plants, including box (*Buxus sempervirens*), erect varieties of rosemary, myrtle (*Myrtus communis*), *Pittosporum tobira* and bay laurel (*Laurus nobilis*).

Whether they are in your own garden, or 'borrowed' from the surrounding landscape, it adds tremendously to the scene if trees like the umbrella pine, date palm and a few Italian cypresses can break the skyline either close-by or in the distance.

ABOVE: The trompe l'oeil mural adds depth to and creates a focal point for the terrace of this garden. The restrained use of both bedding and potted plants (iris, geranium and wisteria) adds to the success of the scheme.

RIGHT: An ideal area for relaxing out of the heat of the midday sun has been created by this colonnade pergola overgrown with a luxuriant grape vine.

The Mediterranean Garden

Agarden bed retained by a rough field-stone wall has been planted at the edge of a
terrace tiled in terracotta, above which a roof is supported by plain white columns. The
plants chosen, although found in Mediterranean climates, are not necessarily natives of the
Mediterranean region. Full use of the columns has been made as a support for climbing
plants, which not only look attractive but also provide shade.

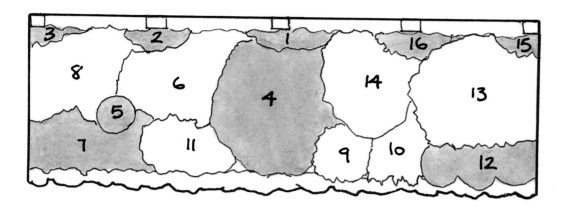

Key to planting scheme

1. *Jasminum polyanthum* climbing to 6m (20ft)

2. *Clematis armandii* (evergreen clematis) climbing to 5m (16ft)

3. *Vitis vinifera* (grape vine) climbing to 6m (20ft)

4. *Ceanothus impressus* 'Puget Blue' (California lilac) height 2m (6ft), spread 1.5 m (5ft)

5. *Citrus limonum* (lemon tree) height 1.5m (5ft), spread 1.2m (4ft)

6. *Cistus x corbariensis* (rock rose) (plant two) height 1.5m (5ft)

7. *Ligularia dentata* height 1.2m (4ft)

8. *Zantedeschia aethiopica* (arum lily) (plant 20) height 1m (3ft)

9. *Rosmarinus* 'Severn Sea'(rosemary) height 1.m (3ft) spread 1.2m (4ft)

10. *Iris germanica* (flag iris) (plant 20) height 60cm (2ft)

11. *Lavandula stoechas* (French lavender) (plant four) height 30cm (1ft)

12. *Sarcococca humilis* (sweet box) (plant three) height 45cm (18in)

13. *Callistemon pallidus* (bottlebrush) height 2m (6ft) spread 1.5m (5ft)

14. *Osmanthus fragrans* (fragrant olive) height 2m (8ft)

15. *Trachelospermum jasminoides* (star jasmine) climbing to 5m (16ft)

16. *Rosa banksiae* climbing to 4m (13ft)

The Seaside Garden

Making a seaside garden, either near a beach or on a headland or clifftop, can be an exciting if challenging experience and involves using radically different plants from those you might plant a few kilometres, or even a few hundred metres, further inland.

In seaside locations, the gardener's great enemy is sea salt, which not only burns the leaves of plants but also, when in the soil, prevents the roots from absorbing water and leads to the death of the plant.

It is the wind which carries the salt from the sea to the plants. Prevailing winds are a constant phenomenon that many plants can come to terms with. It is the very strong gales, which can carry salt great distances inland, that cause the greatest damage to plants. These gales tear leaves and branches to shreds. You can lessen their effects of gales by planting windbreaks between the sea and the main part of your garden.

Many people who live in seaside towns or cities may not have the space to plant deep belts of trees to act as windbreaks but will have sufficient space to put in a single line of trees. These, planted a short distance apart, provide good shelter. Any sort of screen, whether of plants, or made by constructing a fence, will give greater protection if it is permeable. A barrier of wooden slats will give greater protection down-wind than a solid wall of the same height. And a line of closely planted deciduous trees will be more efficient during the winter months when the trees have lost their leaves than in the summer when they are in full leaf. It is for this reason, that trees used as a windbreak, are best planted a tree-width apart.

As Hugo Latymer says in his book, *The Coastal Gardener*, "It can be said in general terms that a barrier that is 40% permeable will reduce wind speed by a half or more for a distance equal to ten times its height to leeward and equal to its height to windward...to be efficient, the barrier must have a length more than twenty times its height if possible and never less than twelve times."

Hedges are also excellent windbreaks. Obviously a loose hedge of tamarind trees will be a more efficient windbreak than a

LEFT: The low horizontal drifts of plants in the foreground interestingly mimic the sea.

hedge of a more compact plant like *Drimys winteri*. On aesthetic grounds, however, you may prefer a solid hedge to the most highly efficient windbreak possible.

Take care in choosing plants for a seaside garden as many trees, shrubs and flowers languish near the sea, just managing to hold on to life. This gives the garden a forlorn and depressing air. It is far better to eliminate such doubtful plants and to concentrate on those that will love the harsh conditions and thrive. While many of the plants that do best by the sea are rather leathery and austere looking, others have an appealing softness and an air of fragility about them. Amongst these are rosemary, lavender, sea bugloss (*Anchusa azurea*), Hibiscus 'Apricot Beauty', escallonia, *Rosa rugosa* and *Fuchsia magellanica*.

LEFT: Harmony is created by all the elements in this garden: the white agapanthus, the balcony, the trellis-work, the leaves of the pandanus trees and the mountain peak seen across the sea.

RIGHT: A carpet of Drosanthemum floribundum *creates an extremely simple but effective garden at the edge of the ocean. Massed planting can create a dramatic visual effect.*

The Seaside Garden

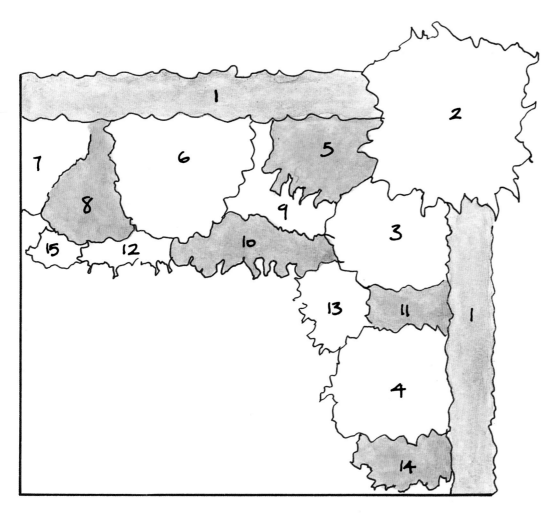

Key to planting scheme

1. *Drimys winteri* (winter bark) height to 6m (20ft)
2. *Tamarix tetranda* (tamarisk) height to 4m (13ft)
3. *Hibiscus* 'Apricot Beauty' height 3m (10ft)
4. *Pittosporum tobira* (Japanese mock orange) height 6m (20ft)
5. *Fuchsia magellanica* height to 1m (3ft)
6. *Escallonia macrantha* height to 3m (10ft)
7. *Ceanothus griseus horizontalis* height to 1.2m (4ft)
8. *Chrysanthemum frutescens* (Canary islands daisy bush; marguerite) height to 1.2m (4ft)
9. *Agapanthus africanus* (agapanthus; Lily-of-the-Nile) height 1m (3ft)
10. *Bergenia cordifolia* height 25cm (10in)
11. *Eryngium maritimum* (sea holly) height to 60cm (2ft)
12. *Coprosma x kirkii* (mirror plant) height to 60cm (2ft)
13. *Lavandula stoechas* (French lavender) height to 30cm (1ft)
14. *Anchusa azurea* (alkanet; summer forget-me-not) height 30cm (1ft)
15. *Centaurea hypoleuca* 'John Coutes' height 60cm (2ft)

A hedge tolerant of salt spray has been planted just above the ocean to give the plants in the garden bed a chance to become established in relatively windless and salt-free conditions. The tamarisk tree is growing above the hedge, partly because it is tolerant of coastal conditions but also because the hedge enables it to establish itself. The other plants were chosen in the hope that the largest of them would also eventually be able to break the line of the hedge.

GARDEN
ARCHITECTURE

Paving Materials

ABOVE: Imaginative Spanish paving using bricks and tiles.
OPPOSITE: Since this terrace is an outdoor room in which to live and entertain, great attention should be paid to the paving materials.

Good garden architecture, for want of a better expression, is always well conceived and constructed, but should never draw undue attention to itself. In all but very exceptional cases, paving, walls, paths and steps are best if understated in their design and construction. Their purpose is to be solid, reassuring and functional.

The cardinal rule is to use local materials wherever possible. In those country areas where stone lies on top of the ground, use local stone for paving and for building walls. In areas where there is underlying clay, such as on the floor of stoneless valleys, use bricks. And in forests and heavily wooded country, consider building timber decks rather than constructing masonry terraces. In the days before the railways, when it was virtually impossible to move building materials in bulk outside their region of origin, houses and gardens were built necessarily of local materials and immediately achieved a unity with their surroundings. Remember that the paving materials will have a strong visual impact and serve the

PREVIOUS PAGE: A summerhouse well clothed with climbers including clematis gives this garden a romantic focal point.

purpose of easing the transition from house to garden.

When using stone for paving, you will have to decide between sawn rectangular stone slabs and crazy paving. Sawn stone tends to be expensive, but crazy paving, particularly if the stones have been purposely smashed, can look busy and unnatural. Gravel is an inexpensive solution but requires regular maintenance.

Having chosen your paving materials, make sure that they are well laid and well drained. When laying the paving of paths and terraces ensure that they have a slight and all but imperceptible tilt so that they shed water efficiently.

Walls and Hedges

Because most gardens today tend to be inward-looking rather than outward-looking, both walls and hedges play an important role. Either around the boundary separating your garden from the outside world, or within the garden where they create a sense of mystery by dividing your world into separate compartments, the wall or hedge need be only just higher than the line of sight. Lower than the line of sight, walls and hedges serve to punctuate the ground plan of your garden; in this way they make a pattern of garden beds into a parterre, or serve to bring a huge lawn into scale with a small house.

Unfortunately, walls are expensive to build. If you have the energy and patience to learn to build them yourself, you can find this a profoundly satisfying experience, as did Sir Winston Churchill, among whose hobbies was building brick walls. Stone walls—either dry or made with cement—are easier to make and just as satisfying.

Hedges are neither as expensive to put in nor as much work as walls, and they have the virtue of being organic. Nothing is a better foil for flowers and foliage than dark hedges such as yew.

Remember though, that hedges need to be clipped from time to time, but there are many that are not labour-intensive and need only be loosely trimmed.

ABOVE: Stone walls lend an air of permanency to a garden and provide a solid support for climbing plants such as this dramatic white hybrid clematis.

OPPOSITE: The straight lines of neatly clipped hedges provides a foil for other, softer, plants.

Paths

The purpose of paths is to provide a secure surface for moving from one place to another around the garden. One path might lead from the street to the front door, and another from the kitchen door to the vegetable patch, for example.

Unless it is your intention that a path visually dwindle out of existence, for example, a path ending in a small wood on the verge of the garden, make certain that the garden paths look business-like, as though they are going somewhere.

The width of a path will depend upon the foot traffic that it could reasonably be expected to bear. You would normally expect the path from the street to the front door to be wider than that leading from the kitchen to the vegetable patch. The minimum width of path that allows two people to walk abreast comfortably is 1.4 metres (4 ft 6 inches). Such a path, or an even wider one, looks logical and right leading to the front door, but in most cases, would look unnaturally wide running to the average vegetable patch.

LEFT: A winding path can give a leisurely air, which suits an informal garden such as this one planted with shrubs, perennials and bulbs.

RIGHT: Unless you intend your garden path to meander out of the line of sight, design it to look as if it is leading somewhere, particularly in a formal garden.

Lawns

Even a very small garden can have a highly successful lawn, provided it is properly designed and maintained. Unfortunately, however, too many garden lawns are failures. They may be too small or too shady and threadbare, or they may have to contend with too many cats and dogs. In such cases it would be better to have some kind of paving instead. To make a positive contribution to your garden, lawns must be healthy and look tidy and this involves a little regular effort.

One of the most difficult things to maintain on a lawn is its edge. If clipped with shears, a tiny bit of earth is invariably sliced away too and, after several years, the flower bed gets progressively larger and the lawn gets progressively smaller. A possible answer is to put in a mowing edge, provided it is discreet. The best materials for this purpose are bricks turned on edge and buried in a sufficiently deep foundation of concrete to ensure that they are not dug up accidentally. If the mowing edge is flush with the lawn, the wheels of the mower can run along its top and there will be no edges to clip afterwards.

ABOVE: *A large sweep of lawn surrounded by tall, established trees such as the one in the photograph above need a lot of maintenance. The same effect can be achieved in a small garden with careful planning.*

OPPOSITE: *A healthy and well-maintained lawn makes the garden inviting. The expanse of lawn emphasises the rock garden in the centre.*

Steps

Because gardens are places in which to relax it helps if the principal flights of steps look generously proportioned and easy to negotiate. Steps with low risers and long treads lend an easy-going air to the garden, whilst those with high risers and narrow treads create an air of effort and tension.

In those gardens built on a steep slope you will be forced to use steps with high risers and narrow treads. In such cases, try not to exceed ten risers before you have a landing, as long, uninterrupted flights of steps can be intimidating. Use handrails only where necessary and always make them as simple as possible. Where a flight of steps passes through, or climbs a retaining wall, make the steps from the same materials as the wall.

In designing the proportions of your steps there is a formula which is very helpful—twice the riser plus the tread equals 65 cm (26 inches). So if you want a 10 cm (4 inch) riser you will need a 45 cm (18 inch) tread. And do not forget to include a 3-6 mm ($^1/_8$) to ($^1/_4$) inch) pitch in the riser dimension so that the steps shed water.

ABOVE: Small ceramic tiles and bricks combine in an imaginative design to make an exciting series of steps.

LEFT: These steps, overgrown with erigeron, impart a marvellous sense of theatre.

Pergolas

In cooler climates pergolas are luxuries, the space for which can probably only be afforded in large gardens, whilst in warmer climates pergolas are almost a necessity in even the smallest garden. In climates with warm sunny winters, lunching out of doors in the dappled shade of a leafless vine growing over a pergola is very pleasant and during the hot summer months, it is the deep shade cast by the vine leaves that makes outdoor dining possible.

The columns of pergolas can be made of wood, brick, stone, metal or concrete, whilst the cross-members, if not made of metal in conjunction with metal uprights, can be made of wood. The combinations of proportion and design are endless, but what is finally decided on will normally be influenced by any nearby house or building. Some pergolas achieve a very pleasing informal effect by having both supports and cross-beams constructed of unsawn natural wooden poles of the same dimensions, whilst others have natural poles as uprights and thick canes of bamboo as cross-beams. A pergola for a formal setting, on the other hand, might have thick round masonry columns contrasting with painted sawn timber cross-beams.

ABOVE: Once the climbing plants cover the pergola and the trellis fence, this New York rooftop garden will gain both privacy from surrounding buildings and shade. Plants in this situation must be chosen for their ability to withstand air pollution!

OPPOSITE: Pergolas smothered with interesting plants such as these rambling roses can transform the small garden. Useful climbers for this purpose include wisteria, jasmine and clematis.

Driveways

The decision as to whether to have a paved or gravel driveway is a personal one based on the look you want to achieve for your property. Paved driveways can look too neat, whereas gravel drives—or even dirt ones—will lend a pleasantly rural air to any town setting. On steep sites where gravel would be washed away by rain or where traction might be more difficult during rain or snow, obviously a paved drive is the logical solution.

On more level sites where both options are open to you, the look of the garden should dictate the type of drive used. A woodland garden will be enhanced by a dirt track and even the most casual of gravel driveways might seem too formal. A very formal garden demands a raked gravel driveway with tidy verges. Such a driveway needs constant mantenance but it is worth the effort for the look of it. Or, you may decide to put down cobble stones instead.

Rectangles of sawn stone are terrific if the setting is right and the budget permits, or, where all else fails, good honest concrete makes a reliable driveway.

White-painted gates swing open to reveal a driveway curving through overhanging trees. Shade-loving rhododendrons provide strong colour.

Decorative Elements

When planning where to place trees and shrubs and flower borders it is also time to consider the kinds of decorative elements that will be appropriate to your scheme.

Certain gardens, particularly formal ones, demand additional decorative elements such as statues and fountains. Consider carefully whether adding such garden ornaments will make a positive contribution to your scheme. After all, it is what is hinted at and left unsaid that is usually more important in garden design rather than extravagent overstatement.

The placing of any garden ornament is important. When choosing a piece, take note of its height and width, then look carefully at the scale of the area where it is to be placed. Make sure it is not too big for the space itself, and the planting surrounding it—does the statue cast too big a shadow over the flowers? Will the climbing plant grow quickly enough to cover its base? Or will it grow too quickly and smother the statue or urn altogether? Garden ornaments act as eye-stoppers in the garden. Position them at the end of a path or axial line for example, to create a focal point.

Wall sculptures come in a wide variety of forms and are suitable for gardens of all sizes, particularly courtyards. A spouting lion's head placed over a small circular pool is one of the more popular forms. Use discretion when choosing and placing a sculpture or piece of garden architecture in your garden, remembering that the basic aim is to create harmony.

Terracotta limed walls are the perfect foil for the cherub's head. The three small pots complete the scene.

INTRODUCING WATER TO THE LANDSCAPE

Ponds and Streams

Nothing in the garden has greater power to intrigue than water. Whether it is a small natural-looking pond at the bottom of the garden, or a gargoyle on a wall spurting water into a small formal pool, both the sight and sound of water capture our imagination. If we catch sight of a jet of water glistening in the sun or hear it gurgling mysteriously somewhere out of sight, we are compelled to explore and discover its source. It is almost as though water is a living thing, with as infinite a range of personality and spirit as the ways we can use it.

Every designer is tempted to add water to the garden. No garden is so tiny that it cannot have a small pond, or a raised tank with a fountain that may sim-

OPPOSITE: In general, the simpler the treatment of water in a garden, the more powerful the effect. Massed waterside plantings of iris add colour.

PREVIOUS PAGE: Using water in the garden adds a further dimension, that of reflection.

ply bubble on the surface. On the other hand, in a larger garden, you may decide to make a large circular pond with a carved stone rim and a central jet of water, the height of which can be regulated at will. Floodlit at night by underwater lights, such a pond can look extremely attractive.

Water has such a powerful presence that it normally demands to be made the focal point of any garden scene. A fountain placed close to a flower bed usually makes too rich a visual feast, unless by your planning you have made it quite clear that the flowers take second place to the water. You will usually find if you attempt to ignore this natural law that the water will upstage your scheme anyhow and give the garden a confused and unresolved appearance. This is so, even if the water is only a small natural-looking pond in a corner at the bottom of the garden. No matter how splendid the statue you might place nearby, it is the water and its reflections that will capture the eye and hold the attention, so let the surface of the small pond take its natural place as the focal point of

that particular part of the garden. Trees overhanging the water will create reflections and a subtle sense of mystery. Make certain that the chosen planting scheme and the general layout of the garden along the line of sight to the water, support your theme of a pond, however obliquely.

On a sloping site you might be tempted to create an artificial stream that tumbles through the garden and which, by means of a pump, repeats the circuit ad infinitum. By installing a balance tank either underground or somewhere out of sight, water lost by evaporation can be replaced from the mains supply. Such an artificial stream can give a strong purpose to a garden that might otherwise be struggling for an identity. It is important, however, that the water does not rush down the slope like some kind of perpetual express train, detracting from the garden's sense of calm. Create waterfalls and pools, so that the water course not only has restful passages here and there in its course, but it also has different cadences at different parts of its course.

Swimming Pools

In choosing and designing the site for a swimming pool both practical and aesthetic considerations need to be taken into account.

From a practical point of view it is important that the swimming pool be exposed to as much sun as possible. There is nothing worse than swimming in a pool in shade on a sunny day. To avoid this, the pool should face south in the northern hemisphere and in the southern hemisphere it should face north. While it is important to have shade trees strategically placed in the garden and around the swimming pool, do not plant them where they will overshadow the pool when they are fully grown. Many people in Australia, California and the Mediterranean region purposely avoid planting eucalypts close to pools because these trees shed leaves year round, posing a never-ending problem of maintenance. Leaves will always be a problem as far as swimming pools are concerned and a compromise is probably the only sensible solution. It is therefore wise to plant a mixture of evergreen and deciduous trees, evergreens because they do not constantly drop large numbers of leaves, and deciduous trees because they shed leaves only once a year. In this way, although there will be several weeks during autumn when you will be busy removing leaves from the filter, the remainder of the year should be comparatively maintenance-free.

Just as sunlight is important to your enjoyment of the swimming pool, so too is lack of wind. Summer is the season you will use your pool the most and it helps if you are aware of the direction of the prevailing wind and can make plans to soften its impact even before you have started the construction of the pool. Perhaps you will plant a tree or a shrub border on the side of the pool affected, to slow down the prevailing wind. Or perhaps you will site the pool so that the bulk of the house provides the needed protection but without creating an undue amount of shade. Finally, you might decide to place your swimming pool inside its own walled or hedged courtyard. This will not only solve the problem of wind, but will also mean you can isolate the pool by means of self-locking doors or gates thus preventing young children from gaining access to it.

Where space and budget permit, build a separate shower and changing room close to the pool, and a small kitchen for preparing snacks. Putting in an extension for the telephone here also means that people do not need to trudge through the house every time the telephone rings.

In designing your swimming pool make sure that the surrounding terrace is wide enough at the deep end to enable swimmers to make a run before diving in. Choose a non-slip paving material for the terrace and, of course, ensure that there is enough space for people to lie down and sunbathe.

One of the main aesthetic questions to consider in designing a swimming pool is that precise point where the surrounding terrace meets the water. Wherever possible, design your pool so that the material of the terrace runs right to the water's edge without an intervening line of concrete or aggregate, and ensure that any tilting and sloping of the surface to ease the draining of water is imperceptible. Your swimming pool will be much more attractive if the terrace flows smoothly and uninterruptedly to the very edge of the water.

Probably the most important of all aesthetic considerations in deciding upon and designing the site for a swimming pool is the fact that it is a sporting installation and difficult to reconcile with many settings. While it can be happily allied to many contemporary styles of architecture, it can be sharply at odds with many others. If the swimming pool, designed as the focal point of the surrounding terrace or garden, is an integral feature of a contemporary house, it can create an interesting sense of harmony. If, however, a contemporary style of pool is seen in close proximity to, say, a Georgian house, the result may be an unfortunate contrast.

Unless you decide upon a very dark lining for your swimming pool, as a design feature to make it seem more ornamental rather than functional, it is probably best to use a white or off-white lining. A white lining enables the pool to reflect the sky and its changing moods in as true a fashion as possible. It always seems incongruous to see pools with light-green or blue linings falsely reflecting a blue sky on what is, in fact, an overcast day.

If your house looks out on to a range of mountains, across a wooded valley or on to a pastoral scene of great beauty, placing your swimming pool anywhere in the main line of sight of such a view will divert attention away from the pool in an unsettling way. Try and site the pool in a sunny corner of the garden where it alone can be the focal point of attention.

The shape of your pool is also very important. Obviously if you intend to swim for exercise and doing laps is your reason for having one, it makes sense to choose a simple rectangle. Likewise, if a pool is to fit inside a walled enclosure or within any kind of rectilinear or formal pattern, a rectangle or oval are probably the best shapes to consider. On a sloping site, however, where it could be attractive for the pool to wrap around the contour of the land, a free-form pool might be the answer. Similarly, if you have chosen to make a subtropical paradise garden, you might decide to all but lose your pool in the centre of a self-made jungle. In such a case, a free-form pool would look far

The swimming pool is enclosed at the far end by a mirrored bricked wall which appears to double the size of the garden. An air of mystery is created by using a dark pool lining.

more natural than a rectangular one.

Indeed, if you have a backyard garden without any particularly interesting view, you might consider making both it and the swimming pool, your view. Choose either a very dark lining or an extremely light one to make your swimming pool look as much like a natural pool as possible. If your pool has a free-form shape, repeat this geometry in the shapes of the beds and plant them with flowing drifts of trees and shrubs. In a colder climate, you could create a forest of trees such as birches, alders and a few conifers, and locate your swimming pool in a clearing amongst them. In a warmer climate, perhaps plant a jungle of banana trees, hibiscus, strelitzias and palms. The important thing is to use your ingenuity to turn the backyard into your view.

SELECTING PLANTS

This section of the book lists plants that are suitable for the various types of garden from the formal to the seaside. It is important to point out that the plants suggested are only a small part of what is both suitable and available. In drawing up a list of new plants for your garden choose ones that will be ecologically compatible with the ones already growing that you intend to retain.

Many of the plants listed are interchangeable between sections. It is possible, for instance, to make a desert garden in a Mediterranean climate. You should be warned, however, that the plants suggested in this chapter for the seaside garden may not necessarily suit the particular climate and exposure of your seaside region. Your own local nurseries will be able to give you further help.

One of this book's most important messages is that in any colour scheme for the garden the leaves of plants are just as important as the flowers. Do not use flower colour simply for the sake of colour. Certainly experiment, but never be afraid of correcting your mistakes. Look critically at your garden to determine how far what you have done works and how you might make improvements in the future.

OPPOSITE: Low, clipped hedging borders a formal vegetable and herb garden.

PREVIOUS PAGE: Japanese wisteria carefully trained around two pillars, over a low-growing bed of mixed azaleas.

THE FORMAL GARDEN

All plants listed below are suitable for clipping and pruning into hedges.

Large

Acer campestre	Field maple
Buxus sempervirens	Common box
Callistemon sp.	Bottlebrush
Camellia sasanqua	
Carpinus betulus	Common hornbeam
Drimys winteri	Winter bark
Escallonia sp.	
Fagus sylvatica	European beech
Ilex aquifolium	English holly
Laurus nobilis	Bay laurel
Pittosporum tobira	
Prunus lusitanica	Portuguese laurel
Taxus baccata	English yew (used in Europe)
Taxus x media 'Hicksii'	Hicks' yew (used in USA)

Small and Medium

Berberis sp.	Barberry
Buxus balearica	Balearic Islands box
Buxus microphylla	Small leaf box
Buxus sempervirens	
'Suffruticosa'	Edging box
Choisya ternata	Mexican orange blossom
Elaeagnus x ebbingei	
Lavandula sp.	Lavender
Myrtus communis	Common myrtle
Rosa rugosa	
Rosmarinus officinalis	Common rosemary
Santolina sp.	
Teucrium chamaedrys	
Viburnum tinus	Laurustinus
Westringia fruticosa	

THE WILD GARDEN

The plants listed in this section are suitable for a wild garden in a temperate climate, particularly the northern United States and Canada.

Large

Alnus sp.	Alder
Amelanchier canadensis	Snowy mespilus, Shadbush
Betula sp	Birch
Carya ovata	Shagbark hickory
Cornus florida 'Rubra'	Dogwood
Juglans nigra	Black walnut
Pinus strobus	White pine
Pterocarya x rehderana	Wingnut
Quercus rubra	Red oak

Medium

Euonymus sp.	
Forsythia sp.	Forsythia
Hydrangea sp.	Hydrangea
Ilex sp.	Holly
Philadelphus sp.	Mock orange
Symphoricarpos sp.	Snowberry
Syringa	Lilac
Viburnum sp.	Viburnum

Small

Convallaria majalis	Lily-of-the-valley
Digitalis sp.	Foxglove
Lysimachia clethroides	
Matteucia struthiopteris	Ostrich fern
Mertensia virginica	Virginia bluebells
Narcissus bulbocodium	Daffodil
Rodgersia podophylla	
Tradescantia virginiana	Spiderwort
Trillium grandiflorum	
Vinca minor	Lesser periwinkle

THE WILD GARDEN (CONT.)

Climbing

Aristolochia durior	Dutchman's pipe
Clematis sp.	
Hedera	Ivy
Lonicera	Honeysuckle
Rosa 'Kiftsgate'	

THE COTTAGE GARDEN

Because cottage gardens by their nature are a haphazard collection of plants, it does not really matter which ones you use provided they give you pleasure. There are some annuals and perennials, however, that are traditionally associated with cottage gardens.

Acanthus mollis	Bear's breeches
Achillea	Yarrow
Aconitum	Monkshood
Alchemilla mollis	Lady's mantle
Alstroemeria	Peruvian lily
Alcea rosea	Hollyhocks
Amaranthus caudatus	Love-lies-bleeding
Anchusa azurea	Alkanet
Antirrhinum majus	Snapdragon
Aquilegia	Columbine
Campanula	Canterbury bell
Centranthus ruber	Valerian
Chelone obliqua	Turtlehead
Cimicifuga racemosa	Black snake-root
Dahlia	Dahlia
Delphinium	Delphinium
Dianthus	Pinks
Dianthus	Carnation
Dianthus barbatus	Sweet William
Dicentra eximia	Fringed bleeding heart
Eremurus robustus	Foxtail lily
Euphorbia	Spurge

THE COTTAGE GARDEN (Cont.)

Foeniculum vulgare	Fennel
Geranium	Cranesbill
Gypsophila paniculata	Baby's breath
Kniphofia	Red-hot-poker
Lupinus	Lupins
Lychnis coronaria	Rose campion
Matthiola	Stock
Nepeta x faassenii	Catmint
Polygonatum multiflorum	Solomon's seal
Scabiosa caucasica	Pincushion flower

THE SMALL BACKYARD GARDEN

The list of plants that would suit a backyard garden, even the smallest one, is endless. Here are some suggestions for both cold and warm climates. Many of these plants do best on acid soil.

TEMPERATE

Large

Cercidyphyllum japonicum	Katsura tree
Cornus nuttallii	Mountain dogwood
Nothofagus antarctica	Antarctic beech
Ostrya japonica	Japanese hop hornbeam
Oxydendron arboreum	Sorrel tree
Pyrus ussuriensis	Manchurian pear

Medium

Berberis sp.	Barberry
Exochorda racemosa	Pearlbush
Osmanthus delavayi	
Rubus tridel 'Benenden'	Ornamental bramble
Sarcococca hookerana	Sweet box
Sarcococca humilis	Sweet box

THE SMALL BACKYARD GARDEN (CONT.)

Small

Alchemilla mollis	Lady's mantle
Astilbe	
Hosta sp.	Plantain lily
Iris sp.	Catmint
Nepeta	

Climbing

Clematis sp.	
Hydrangea petiolaris	Climbing hydrangea
Jasminum sp.	Jasmine
Lonicera	Honeysuckle
Wisteria sinensis	Wisteria

SUBTROPICAL

Large

Gordonia axillaris	
Magnolia heptapeta	Yulan
Michelia doltsopa	
Prunus persica	Peach

Medium

Boronia megastigma	Scented boronia
Camellia sasanqua	
Fortunella japonica	Marumi cumquat
Gardenia augusta 'Professor Pucci'	
Rhododendron indicum 'Alba Magna'	Azalea 'Alba Magna'

Climbing

Actinidia chinensis	Chinese gooseberry
Clematis armandii	
Thunbergia grandiflora	Bengal clock vine
Trachelospermum jasminoides	Star jasmine
Wisteria sinensis	Wisteria

THE LOW MAINTENANCE GARDEN

Low maintenance gardens can be made in cool climates and in warmer ones. Listed below are plants for both temperate and subtropical climates.

TEMPERATE

Large

Acer sp.	Maple
Magnolia sp.	
Mespilus germanica	Medlar
Prunus sargentii	Sargent's cherry
Sorbus aria 'Lutescens'	Whitebeam

Medium

Berberis sp.	Barberry
Daphne odora	
Hebe rakaiensis	Veronica
Rhododendron sp.	
Viburnum davidii	

Small

Bergenia cordifolia	Pig squeak
Epimedium sp.	Barrenwort
Lamium maculatum	Spotted dead nettle
Pulmonaria angustifolia	Lungwort

Climbing

Actinidia chinensis	Chinese gooseberry
Clematis	
Lonicera sp.	Honeysuckle
Vitis vinifera	Grape vine

SUBTROPICAL

Large

Acmena smithii	Lilly Pilly
Ficus hillii	
Howea fosterana	Kentia palm
Lagerstroemia indica	Crepe myrtle
Michelia champaca	

SUBTROPICAL (Cont.)

Medium

Boronia megastigma	Scented boronia
Brunfelsia australis	Morning-noon-and-night
Grevillea hookerana	Hooker's grevillea
Murraya paniculata	Cosmetic bark tree
Rondeletia amoena	Pink rondeletia

Small

Asplenium australe	Bird's nest fern, Spleenwort
Convolvulus mauritanicus	Ground morning glory
Polianthes tuberosa	Tuberose
Zebrina pendula	
Zephyranthes candida	

Climbing

Allamanda cathartica	Allamanda
Aristolochia elegans	Dutchman's pipe
Gelsemium sempervirens	Carolina jasmine
Stephanotis floribunda	Madagascar jasmine
Thunbergia alata	Black-eyed Susan

THE DESERT GARDEN

The plants listed here are all suitable for desert or dry gardens. Most, but not all will not tolerate too much moisture.

Large

Beaucarnea recurvata	Ponytail
Chamaerops humilis	Mediterranean fan palm
Cordyline australis	Cabbage tree
Dracaena draco	Dragon tree
Pandanus utilis	Screw pine
Phoenix roebelenii	Dwarf date palm
Washingtonia robusta	Mexican fan palm
Yucca elephantipes	Spineless yucca

THE DESERT GARDEN (Cont.)

Medium

Agave americana	Century plant
Agave attenuata	Swan's neck agave
Aloe arborescens	Tree aloe, Candelabra plant
Aloe marlothii	*Beschorneria yuccoides*
Euphorbia milii	Crown of thorns
Phormium tenax	New Zealand flax
Portulacaria afra	Jade plant, Elephant bush
Yucca gloriosa	Spanish dagger

Small

Echeveria x hybrida	Hens and chickens
Euphorbia caput-medusae	Medusa's head
Kalanchoe blossfeldiana	
Kalanchoe fedtschenkoi	
Senecio serpens	Blue chalksticks
Trichacereus huascha	
Mesembryanthemum	Iceplant
Stapelia gigantea	Carrion flower

Climbing

Epiphyllum	Ochid cactus
Hoya carnosa	Waxflower
Hylocereus undulatus	Nightblooming cereus
Jasminum azoricum	

THE SUBTROPICAL GARDEN

Most of the plants listed here will only thrive in areas in which there is no frost.

Large

Albizia julibrissin 'Rosea'	Pink silk tree
Arecastrum romanzoffianum	Queen palm
Jacaranda mimosifolia	Jacaranda
Livistona australis	Australian fountain palm
Musa sp.	Banana
Phoenix reclinata	

THE SUBTROPICAL GARDEN (Cont.)

Medium

Phyllostachys bambusoides	Bamboo
Plumeria acutifolia	Frangipani
Strelitzia nicolai	Bird-of-Paradise tree
Tipuana tipu	Rosewood
Alpinia nutans	Ginger
Cestrum nocturnum	
Cycas revoluta	Cycad
Brugmansia suaveolens	Angel's trumpet
Gardenia jasminoides	
Hibiscus rosa-sinensis	Hibiscus
Pittosporum tobira	
Raphiolepis indica	Pink Indian hawthorn
Strelitzia reginae	Bird-of-Paradise flower
Tibouchina urvilleana	Glory bush

Small

Agapanthus africanus	Agapanthus, Lily of the Nile
Amaryllis belladonna	Cape belladonna
Canna	Canna lilies
Clivia miniata	Clivia
Cymbidium	Orchid
Erigeron	Fleabane
Impatiens	Impatience
Pelargonium	Ivy leaf geranium
Zantedeschia aethiopica	Arum lily
Ophiopogon	Mondo grass

Climbing

Bougainvillea	
Campsis grandiflora	Chinese trumpet creeper
Mandevilla laxa	Chilean jasmine
Monstera deliciosa	
Podranea ricasoliana	Pink trumpet vine
Thunbergia grandiflora	Bengal clock vine
Trachelospermum jasminoides	Star jasmine

THE MEDITERRANEAN GARDEN

Mediterranean climates exist on most continents in the world and, as a result, many of the plants listed here are not natives of the Mediterranean region.

Large

Acacia sp.	Wattle; mimosa
Arbutus sp.	Strawberry tree
Cercis siliquastrum	Judas tree
Citrus limonum	Lemon tree
Cupressus sempervirens	Italian cypress
Cycas revoluta	Cycad
Olea europea	Olive tree
Phoenix canariensis	Canary Islands palm
Phoenix dactylifera	Date palm
Pinus pinea	Umbrella pine

Medium

Buddleia sp.	Butterfly bush
Callistemon sp.	Bottlebrush
Carpenteria californica	Carpenteria
Ceanothus sp.	California lilac
Cestrum nocturnum	Night jessamine
Choisya ternata	Mexican orange blossom
Cistus sp.	Rock roses
Convolvulus cneorum	Convolvulus, Silverbush
Euphorbia sp.	Spurge
Myrtus communis	Common myrtle

Small

Acanthus mollis	Bear's breeches
Ballota pseudodictamnus	Ballota
Chrysanthemum frutescens	Canary Islands daisy bush
Clivia miniata	Clivia
Cyclamen sp.	Cyclamen
Echium sp.	Echium
Hemerocallis sp.	Day lilies
Iris germanica	Flag iris
Phlomis fruticosa	Jerusalem sage

Climbing

Clematis sp.	Clematis
Kennedia sp.	Kennedia
Rosa sp.	Rose
Vitis vinifera	Grape vine
Wisteria sinensis	Wisteria

THE SEASIDE GARDEN

The plants that you will be able to grow by the sea will depend upon the climate and also upon how exposed your garden is to salt spray and wind. Before actually buying any plants ask the advice of your local nurseries who will be able to give you a reasonable idea of what should succeed in your locality.

Large

Acacia sp.	Wattle; mimosa
Erythrina crista-galli	Coral tree
Eucalyptus gomphocephala	Gum tree
Griselinia sp.	
Metrosideros excelsus	New Zealand Christmas tree
Quercus ilex	Holly oak
Schinus molle	Peppercorn tree
Tamarix sp.	
Washingtonia filifera	Californian fan palm

Medium

Correa backhousiana	
Elaeagnus x ebbingei	
Hibiscus cv. 'Apricot Beauty'	
Hibiscus syriacus	Rose-of-Sharon
Myoporum laetum	
Nerium oleander	Oleander
Pistacia sp.	Pistachio
Pittosporum tobira	Pittosporum
Raphiolepis indica	Indian hawthorn
Teucrium frutescens	

Small

Agapanthus africanus	Agapanthus, Lily-of-the-Nile
Centranthus ruber	Valerian
Echinops ritro	Globe thistle
Eryngium sp.	Sea holly
Eschscholzia californica	
Gazania sp.	Californian poppy
Limonum latifolium	Sea lavender
Mesembryanthemum sp.	Ice plant
Portulacaria afra	Jade plant, Elephant bush
Rosmarinus officinalis	Rosemary

Climbing

Bougainvillea	
Campsis grandiflora	Chinese trumpet creeper
Hedera sp.	Ivy
Jasminum sp.	Jasmine
Trachelospermum jasminoides	Star jasmine

Index

Acknowledgements

To my father

I would like to thank Hugo Latymer for the privilege of reading his book *The Coastal Gardener* in manuscript form, and for his permission to quote from this book. I would also like to thank him for allowing me to research *Creating Style* in his extensive library of horticultural books and for his advice which is always sound.

It is impossible to name here all those people around the world who have allowed photographs of their gardens to appear in this book. I nonetheless thank them all.

Finally I would like to thank my father and Elizabeth Henderson for their patience during those weeks I was writing this book.

PHOTOGRAPHY CREDITS

Front cover Jerry Harpur; Back cover Jerry Harpur; Endpapers Andrew Pfeiffer; Title page Andrew Pfeiffer; p.4 Balthazar Korab; p.5 Jerry Harpur; pp.6–7 Jerry Harpur; p.8 Balthazar Korab; p.9 Jerry Harpur; p.11 Jerry Harpur; pp.12–13 Weldon Publishing; p.14 Weldon Publishing; p.15 Weldon Publishing; p 16 Jerry Harpur; p.17 Andrew Pfeiffer; p.18 Andrew Pfeiffer; p.20 Jerry Harpur; p.22 Balthazar Korab; p.24 Andrew Pfeiffer; p.25 Andrew Pfeiffer; pp. 26–27 Weldon Publishing; p.28 Weldon Publishing; p.30 Andrew Pfeiffer; p.33 Balthazar Korab; pp.34–35 Jerry Harpur; p.36 Jerry Harpur; p.38 Plan drawn by James Pfeiffer; p.39 Balthazar Korab; pp.40–41 Jerry Harpur; p.42 Jerry Harpur; p.46 Balthazar Korab; p.50 Jerry Harpur; p.51 Derek Fell; p.52 Weldon Publishing; p.54 Jerry Harpur; p.55 Jerry Harpur; p.58 Australian Design Series Magazines (ACP Publishing Pty Limited); p.61 Jerry Harpur; p.64 Jerry Harpur; p.65 Gil Hanly; p.67 Jerry Harpur; p.70 Australian Design Series Magazines (ACP Publishing Pty Limited); p.71 Gil Hanly; p.72 top Joyce Oudkerk Pool; p.72 bottom Joyce Oudkerk Pool; p.73 Joyce Oudkerk Pool; p.76 Jerry Harpur; p.77 Weldon Publishing; p.79 Gil Hanly; p.82 Janne Faulkner/Nexus Designs; p.84 Jerry Harpur; p.85 Andrew Pfeiffer; p.88 Jerry Harpur; p.90 Gil Hanly; p.91 Derek Fell; pp.94–95 Derek Fell; p.96 Andrew Pfeiffer; p.97 Andrew Pfeiffer; p.98 Andrew Pfeiffer; p.99 Balthazar Korab; p.100 Jerry Harpur; p.101 Andrew Pfeiffer; p.102 Balthazar Korab; p.103 Weldon Publishing; p.104 Weldon Publishing; p.105 Jerry Harpur; p.106 Andrew Pfeiffer; p.107 Jerry Harpur; p.108 Weldon Publishing; p.109 Jerry Harpur; pp.110–111 Weldon Publishing; p.112 Balthazar Korab; p.115 Weldon Publishing; pp.116–117 Jerry Harpur; p.118 Balthazar Korab

A Kevin Weldon Production

Published by Weldon Publishing
a division of Kevin Weldon & Associates Pty Limited
70 George Street, Sydney NSW 2000, Australia

First published in the United Kingdom in 1992 by
ANAYA Publishers Ltd
3rd floor, 50 Osnaburgh Street, London NW1 3ND

Project editor: Deborah Nixon
Copy editor: Shirley Jones
Designer: Kathie Baxter Smith

Designed on Quark Express in 11.5pt Garamond 3
Printed in Australia by Griffin Press, Adelaide

British Library Cataloguing in Publication Data

Pfeiffer, Andrew
Creating Style – (Pleasure of Gardening Series)
I. Title II. Series
635
ISBN 1 – 85470 – 144 – 4

*Front cover: Strong architectural features provide the basic framework around which the garden has been
designed. Established trees provide the backdrop.*

*Back cover: A garden framed by bowers of climbing roses and a pathway edged with lavender
fronting mixed perennial beds.*

*Endpapers: A parterre garden of clipped box and yew hedges create a formal pattern in a
Michigan garden.*

Title page: The herb garden at Sissinghurst is a delight at the height of the English summer.

*Opposite contents page: It is important to isolate a formal garden from its surroundings. Here, a dark green
yew hedge isolates the formal part of the garden from the natural plantation of trees beyond.*

*Contents page: The violet and magenta flowers of Allium aflatunense and Polemonium harmonise
well together because they are next to each other on the colour spectrum. Blue and magenta together
without violet to bridge the gap would be less harmonious.*